The understanding of faith

THE UNDERSTANDING
OF FAITH

Interpretation and criticism

Edward Schillebeeckx

Translated by N. D. Smith

A Crossroad Book

The Seabury Press · New York

The Seabury Press
815 Second Avenue
New York, N.Y. 10017

Originally published as *Geloofsverstaan* by
H. Nelissen, Bloemendaal, Holland 1972
Copyright © Sheed and Ward 1974
Printed in the United States of America

LIBRARY OF CONGRESS CATALOGING IN PUBLICATION DATA

Schillebeeckx, Edward Cornelis Florentius Alfons,
   1914–
   The understanding of faith: interpretation and
criticism.

   "A Crossroad book."
   Translation of Geloofsverstaan.
   Includes bibliographical references.
   1. Theology—Addresses, essays, lectures.
   2. Hermeneutics—Addresses, essays, lectures.
   I. Title.
   BR85.S274313   201'.1   74–12465
   ISBN 0–8164–1185–9

CONTENTS

INTRODUCTION

During the last five or so years, the hermeneutic question, that is, the question of how the christian message should be interpreted nowadays, has come to assume a central position in catholic theology. Although the difficulties involved in this interpretation were not unknown before, it is only fairly recently that we have come to realise that we can no longer try to understand scripture or the church's dogmas on the basis of our previous presuppositions. In other words, the theoretical pre-understanding which we have up till now taken as our point of departure has been broken down into a very great number of presuppositions which are not identical and which may even be contradictory. This has brought to light the urgent need for attention to be given to the possibilities and the limits of an understanding of faith that is both creative and faithful to the gospel.

Two basic problems can be classified under the heading of theological hermeneutics. First, how can a christian who believes in the biblical message of the kingdom of God understand this message in the twentieth century and how can he justify this new, contemporary interpretation as a christian understanding? Secondly, how can he, within the many different religious and non-religious interpretations of the world and of human life which surround him, justify his christian interpretation of reality with regard to modern thought or at least when faced with the legitimate demands of modern thinking?

I shall deal with each of these two problems, which are fundamental to theological hermeneutics, in separate collections of essays. Most of the contributions in the present volume are related to the first of these two problems. It includes articles written over the past six years, a time during which hermeneutics were still in their infancy in catholic theology, and the whole territory was still being explored.

The earlier chapters, 1–5, approach the question of how we are to know if a new interpretation of the christian message or of an earlier dogma, for example, the dogma of original sin as defined at the Councils of Orange and Trent or that of Christ's two natures at Chalcedon, is really faithful to the gospel and thus orthodox? In these chapters I have tried to show that, although theoretical elements of faith are involved in this question, no purely theoretical solution can be found. What is more, not only the content of faith, but also the continuity of faith—which has until recently generally been approached as a question of the development of dogma, but is now usually treated as a question whether a given interpretation is or is not an actualisation which is faithful to the gospel—ultimately belong to faith itself and not to mere theoretical verification. This continuity is, after all, faith in its contemporary articulation; otherwise, it is a misrepresentation of faith. In other words, the correctness of this actualising theology, which seeks to continue and make present the christian interpretation of reality, cannot be demonstrated in purely theoretical terms or by purely historical or logical argument.[1]

On the other hand, however, it should be borne in mind that it is not the theologians of the church, but believers themselves in the christian community who make revelation present here and now by their faith and by making the christian revelation their own. This faith here and now brings revelation into the *saeculum* of the twentieth century. Revelation is only made present in and through the secularising act of faith and this is inevitably an act made here and now. It therefore comes within the conditions imposed by contemporary criticism. How could a definition of faith proclaimed several centuries after the original event of Christ's revelation, for example, at Chalcedon in the fifth century AD, be a dogma, an official expression of revelation, unless it were the secularisation of the event of Christ's revelation, that is, the bringing of that revelation into the *saeculum* of the fifth century? The present thus enters into the appropriation, by understanding, of revelation itself. This act of appropriation and therefore of making faith present and actual is the act of faith itself, of which the only criterion is faith, just as the 'why' of faith is not knowing, but believing, which can never be fully fathomed by reason.

All the same, the believer is a man who thinks and who is in history. His faith causes him to think. Neither in theory nor in practice can he formulate convincing rational criteria for the 'why' of faith or for the correctness of an interpretation of faith here and now. This does not, however, imply that his faith or his re-interpretation of faith is purely arbitrary. Even rationally, he has prudential reasons and criteria for his faith, with the result that, at the level of reflection, at which he attempts to assure himself of his faith or the correctness of a theological interpretation of that faith here and now, the believer can only rely on a convergence of many different criteria, each of which is insufficient in itself. Neither the separate criteria in themselves nor their sum total can result in an apodictic verification. If, however, we consider the question at the personal level, from the point of view of the sense of faith within the believing community, taking as our point of departure the fact that a 'new' interpretation of faith is accepted by that community as served by the church's teaching office, then we shall have sufficient criteria, even though each criterion may in itself be rationally fallible. In the first place, there are logical and linguistic criteria, which have evolved from progressive philological, historical and exegetical procedures which can also be applied both to the pronouncements of the church's teaching office and to the biblical message. Secondly, we have criteria which are universally hermeneutic and which are given to us in the typical proportional relationship between the various models of interpretation of scripture and tradition, and the text to be interpreted. Finally, there are criteria which bring to light the continuity with the inspiration of the gospel in the act of faith today.

There are two pre-requisites for this whole process of verification. First there is the experiential context of all our concepts of faith and second the recognition that any confession of faith and therefore any contemporary interpretation of faith that is faithful to the gospel must have a doxological character.

Truth is inwardly orientated towards universal consent and

cannot be bound by restricting qualifications. This consent is only relevant when it has come about within the framework of free dialogue. The whole of hermeneutic science is ultimately based on the possibility of mutual understanding or agreement. All that has to be done in the hermeneutic process is to remove breakdowns of communication.

Since the enlightenment, however, we have been explicitly confronted with the fact that institutional structures in society and the power exercised by one section over the rest of society within those structures are able to prevent this general consent or agreement from being reached in the only possible way, that is, on the basis of free dialogue. In other words, the hermeneutic process can be obstructed by institutional structures. All of us have at some time or other experienced, in our immediate environment or outside it, times when we have been almost forced to admit 'it is impossible to talk to people like that'. In other words, we have a sharp experience of the limits of the hermeneutic process. Again we all know how, for instance, during a strike, the hermeneutic process of mutual understanding between employer and employee is blocked by power structures. The need to break through or to change those structures may therefore be an essential aspect of the hermeneutic process, if it is to lead eventually to general consent or to mutual understanding.

Since the time of the enlightenment, then, the conviction that this hermeneutic process cannot be a purely theoretical undertaking has gained ground; it is also seen to have a social and political dimension. What therefore is required by the hermeneutic process on the basis of its fundamental interest in communication is a special emancipative interest in really democratic structures within which free agreement can gradually come about. What has to develop within the hermeneutic process is a practical and critical interest in structures which will make freedom possible. In this sense, then, the process of finding truth and the hermeneutic process of communication and understanding have a political dimension.

The now classical science of hermeneutics is therefore confronted, in the last two chapters of this book, with these recent tendencies which re-examine the relationship between theory and praxis. As an introduction to this new problem, I take several and broadly speaking politically progressive statements made by the church's teaching office as a model, even though the hermeneutic question of the relationship between theory and praxis does not arise sharply or fully in these statements. They are, however, important because they establish a connection between the need for a social policy and a really christian understanding of faith. The new problem is, however, brought sharply into focus by the 'critical theories' of the so-called Frankfurt school (Max Horkheimer and Theodor Adorno and, outside this school, Ernst Bloch) and above all by Jürgen Habermas. (The perspective from which these authors write is not, of course, christian, but unmistakably secularised old testament Jewish.) Habermas' difficulties with the Frankfurt school show how undeveloped but at the same time how urgent the whole problem is at present. Many different forms of the critical theory of society have evolved in recent years and these have, directly or indirectly, inspired younger theologians, who have described their views as, for example, 'critical catholicism', 'critical christianity' or 'contestation'. In addition to this, various forms of 'political theology' have also been developed.

What interests me above all at the moment in all these tendencies is whether they really contain elements which have been overlooked by the science of hermeneutics and thus by philosophical and theological hermeneutics in their reflection about themselves. In his study of the critical theories of society and political contestation, then, the theologian may for this reason be led to examine his own conscience in a reflection which is bound to yield more positive results than a firm intention to embellish completed theological treatises with elements criticising society, rather as 'pious corollaries' were added in the past to theological analyses. Theological reflection about the contribution that can be made by these new movements may lead theologians to conclude that the christian message can be handed down in a contemporary interpretation if theology can act as the reflective and critical self-consciousness of christian praxis. In this, theology can not only interpret the reality of faith, but also formulate operational models in order to renew faith, and thus lay the foundation in praxis for the validity of an interpretation here and now of that reality. In this way, a new relationship between theory and practice will be brought to light in theology.

E. SCHILLEBEECKX op

The understanding of faith

I
THE INTERPRETATION OF THE FUTURE

The christian believes that the living God showed the uniqueness and power of his unconditional love for man in Jesus Christ, and thus revealed himself as man's salvation. The first christian generations confessed this event and expressed this confession in many varied ways in the books of the new testament. These books, therefore, give us interpretations of the Jesus-event against the background of the old testament sphere of understanding.

The dialectic of the development of dogma or tradition shows that, in order to be faithful to the original event, the church was constantly obliged to give a fresh interpretation of this apostolic interpretation. This problem became acute for the first time when christianity with its Palestinian culture and corresponding interpretation was transplanted to an environment with a Hellenistic culture and mentality. The new testament still shows clear traces of the difficulties experienced in this 'translation'.

I An interpretation of an interpretation
We listen to this message now, in our own age. And this means that in our different situation and our different sphere of understanding we react to this christian message with constant questioning. The relevance, therefore, of the message concerning the ultimate things, the *eschata*, or the final and definitive salvation of man, implies the need to analyse our own sphere of understanding, not only from the point of view of the

sociology and philosophy of our own culture, but also theologically. But, precisely because our modern self-understanding carries our whole past with it, we cannot grasp our present
sphere of understanding if we do not take equal care to understand our own past. To try to assimilate the eschatological
message of the bible today without a critical understanding
of what theology made of it in the many centuries of its past,
with a constantly changing understanding, would be wholly
inadequate. A first glance at this process shows clearly that the
constantly renewed assimilation of the christian message is
connected with the common expression of changing views on
man and the world, and formulated by a succession of philosophical schools. To examine the differences in understanding
that succeeded each other in the church's two-thousand-year-
old tradition is therefore a hermeneutic requirement in the
interpretation of the christian confession of the *eschata*.

But this same investigation must penetrate into the depths
of the old and new testament origins of this eschatological
confession. This process shows that different cultures clash
with each other and inspire different kinds of question. It also
shows that, while becoming aware of all these differences, the
believer is really trying to interpret and reflect on the meaning
of that phase in history in which he himself lives. The old
testament is then seen as the key source for the explanation
of the life and death of a people who became aware of being
God's people, just as the new testament became the key source
for the explanation of Jesus' life and death. Both the old and
the new testament have an interpretative function: up to a
point they interpret their own content; they are hermeneutics
in action. But for us this collection of writings is itself something in need of interpretation. And so hermeneutics becomes
the interpretation of an interpretation.

Although, then, the problem of interpretation is itself
already one of the facts of the bible, it has become more acute
today than ever before, and this for two main reasons. First,
we no longer belong to the same culture, no longer have the
same mentality or the same outlook on man and the world, as
those that prevailed in the days when the original and the
later interpretations of the Christ-event were formulated. The
distance in time makes our problem far more difficult. The
culture of the Semites and that of Hellenism at least shared
a common 'antiquity'. Yet a modern translation is possible be-

cause the ancient self-understanding of man is one of the elements that has shaped our modern self-understanding. Pluralism is never absolute. Although there is no identity, there are always channels of communication between the various interpretations. Secondly, we belong to an age which acknowledges the demands of textual and historical criticism, an age which considers it immoral to surrender oneself unconditionally to something without some rational justification: all people, including those of good will, reject *a priori* a kind of blind faith which has no human and genuine intelligible basis. Even with our unconditional obedience of faith we can no longer avoid the need to make the eschatological dogmas intelligible and in some way understandable. Today faith insists that the believer pass through the ordeal of a new interpretation of his faith if he wishes to be faithful to the message of the gospel.

II History and the future

Today we observe a basic shift in the way man looks at history. The more or less explicit identification of history with the past, which dominated the writing of history since the beginning of its modern phase, is now yielding to a view which sees history more as events in the making, events in the process of arrival, and therefore as happenings in which we ourselves play an active part. The future is of primary importance in what we call 'history'. So the concept of man's earthly future begins to exercise a kind of polarity in man's thought and knowledge, whereas in the past—at least in the West—the future dimension of history was almost only considered as a matter of the *finis ultimus*, the ultimate end of man, beyond and after this earthly life.

Since the rediscovery of man's true historicity as a creature of time, that on the basis of its past sets its course of life in the present towards a future, eschatology is seen as a question which lies embodied in man's existence. Man's experience does not simply run on in time, with an undercurrent of 'becoming', but implies an element of time-consciousness. This does not allow him to escape from time but it allows him in a certain sense to transcend the lived time (*le temps vécu*), although he cannot put this time-transcending permanence into words, at least not positively. This time-consciousness which makes man reach beyond experienced time into both the past and the future makes man's questioning about the beginning and the end particularly relevant.

It seems to me, therefore, that to inquire after the future is a natural process, and fundamental to our human condition. Although caught up in time and never outside it, man is not the prisoner of time in his historical growth; he transcends time from within. That is why he can never feel satisfied. Within this time-condition man is therefore free to achieve a certain openness with regard to time. He can do so because he can also indulge like an epicure in the short-lived joys of the temporary condition in which he lives. But if he takes this time-consciousness seriously, he cannot avoid facing the question of the meaning of human history. For every moment of his free existence implies present, past and future. His freedom indeed is exercised in the present but only in so far as this present sets its course towards the future. The pure present is always on the point of sliding into the past. Man's future-building freedom thus essentially presupposes an open eschatology, an expectation of the future, a will towards the future which, in itself, slips into the ambiguity of all history-making freedom.

III The future as transcendence

When in our old culture, mainly concerned with the past, we thought and spoke about God's transcendence we almost naturally projected God into the past. Eternity was something like an immobilised or immortalised past—'in the beginning was God'. We knew of course quite well that God's eternity embraced man's present and man's future; that God was both first and last, and as such also a present that transcended our human present. On this point the older theology developed marvellous insights which have by no means lost their relevance. In a culture which constantly looked towards the past there existed obviously a powerful mutual attraction between 'transcendence' and eternity on the one hand and an immortalised 'past' on the other. Today, however, our culture is firmly turned towards the future as something that our culture itself must build. So the christian notion of transcendence, supple and capable of more than one meaning, has to go through the same process. The meaning of 'transcendence' comes therefore closer to what in our time-bound condition we call 'future'. If divine transcendence transcends and embraces man's past, present and future from within, the believer will preferably and rightly link God's transcendence with the future as soon as man has recognised the primacy of the future in our time-bound condition. So he will link God with the future of man and, since man is a communal person, with the future of mankind as a whole. When we once accept the reality of a genuine belief in the invisible reality of God who is the true source of our understanding of God from within this world, this new understanding of his transcendence will lead to the new image of God in our culture.

In this cultural context the God of the believer will manifest himself as 'He who comes', the God who is our future. This implies a far-reaching change: he, whom we formerly saw as the 'wholly other' in our old outlook on man and the world, is now seen as he who is our future and who creates anew man's future. He shows himself as the God who gives us in Jesus Christ the opportunity to build the future, to make all things new and to rise above our own sinful history and that of all mankind. Thus the new culture becomes an inspiration to rediscover as a surprise the good news of the old and the new testament, the news that the God of promise has put us on the way to the promised land, a land which, like Israel of old, we ourselves must claim and cultivate, trusting in his promise.

IV God's faithfulness

In order to avoid hasty conclusions one should not lose sight of the biblical basis of what I have called this new understanding of God. The new culture is but an occasion and stimulus to rediscover the living God as our future in the old and the new testament. But according to the bible the basis of the eschatological expectation of the future is the certainty, in faith, of an actual relationship with God. This actual relationship with the God of the covenant, which makes the past present again, must not be sacrificed to the primacy of the future. The basis of our hope is therefore our faith in Yahweh who reveals himself in both past and present as the living God of the community.

This is understandable when we realise that the present and its past are the only basis on which we can build a future, otherwise we simply land ourselves in futuristic fantasies. The past belongs essentially to our human condition which in its present is orientated towards the future. And the interpretation of old testament history shows that the past only becomes clearer in the present when again and again it is seen in the light of the future. In the bible the interpretation of a past event always coincides with the announcement of a new expectation for the future. The past is 'read again' in a manner which makes it once more actual, and thus it becomes a guarantee for the hope of a new future.[2] Embodied in the scriptural canon, the traditional material which voices future expectations is raised above the level of its original intent, and in this dimension of its own future the past remains for ever actual. The etiological explanation of the present from the past is at the same time a confession that new salvation is dawning. Thus the critical analysis of the old testament theme of taking possession of the land shows that its connection with the theme of fulfilment and promise is a theological reflection on the *actual* possession of the holy land. Here we have therefore a theological view of history arising from actuality and providing an interpretation of the past as well as a pointer towards the future.

If we want to understand Israel's history as a promise, we shall find that this promise is not an absolute starting-point without a prehistory, as if it were a kind of word of God which promised Israel a new future out of the blue and from on high, and drew a picture of it with all its future and observable features. On the contrary, Israel only began to understand its own history as a divine promise when it looked back from its present to its own past and recognised God's faithfulness, a faithfulness which naturally means an expectation of future salvation for man through history and therefore looks towards the future. Looking back, we see Yahweh's faithfulness as promise; looking ahead, we see it as an expectation and continuous fulfilment, and on the basis of this faithfulness our expectation constantly opens up a new future through a history which stretches beyond us. It is therefore through the historical development of its tradition that Israel began to understand what was meant by God's promise. Because Israel remembered certain meaningful events from the past and associated them with new events of the present, both past and present illuminated each other, and thus it experienced and interpreted its history as the gradual fulfilment of a divine promise. Within this concept of history the present itself was seen as a new promise, a new door opening to a new future. And ultimately the whole earthly history becomes the unfolding of an eschatological expectation.

It is therefore a lived tradition, a history of the transmission of traditions, which underlies the Israelite's interpretation of history as a divine promise, as God's saving activity, as covenant and, implied in all this, as revelation. An event experienced by the community is handed down to future generations only in so far as, and because, it has a special meaning for that community. And the community discovers the meaning of this event because it has passed through a particular history which carries traditions and insights with it. The past event only reaches us, therefore, with the meaning it had for that community and never without it or outside it. The history of the transmission of traditions thus reveals the gradual unfolding of the meaning of the event to future generations, with all the additions and corrections which the constant reading and re-reading of the event have brought to it in the further development of history. We can only discover the meaning of a past event for us now by taking into account also the history of traditions without arbitrary interpretations. We see here the principle of hermeneutics. Only when we understand history as a critically examined history of traditions can we understand it as a promise that was lived in Israel and received its first definitive fulfilment in Jesus Christ.[3]

If we see biblical history as an event handed down to us in a believing and critical interpretation, we can also see that the reference to the future is contained in the present of the people of God as it lives within the context of this history of traditions. 'Future' is an intrinsic dimension of present, is related to what must still happen in time without allowing us to see its future shape at present. This biblical structure of the prophecy of the future which sets the present within a living history of traditions rejects on the one hand any 'de-eschatologisation' of time (there is no room for a radical eschatology of the present) and on the other hand demands a rejection of all apocalyptic elements from the expectation of the future (apocalyptic thought thinks from the future to the present).

Because of man's essential historicity, 'future' means a future starting from the present and therefore from the past. Although its actual shape remains hidden, the future is an intrinsic element in man's self-understanding. This hidden reality is therefore intrinsically related to the actuality. This has been insufficiently understood by Jürgen Moltmann.

In this sense there can be no true eschatology of the future without a certain eschatology of the present. Although the future has an element of 'not yet' in it we cannot neglect the element of 'already'. In fact, only the 'already' allows us to say anything meaningful about the still unknown future. It is therefore typical that the old testament never describes the unknown future in totally new and unexpected terms. Hope always looks for some ideal restoration, the particular features of which are supposed to be known from the past. The total picture, however, is always new. Expectation is not a state of hoping for a simple re-shaping of the past. Israel hoped for the fulfilment of what Yahweh had already done in its desire for the total achievement of it all. The re-actualisation of the past in the present with an eye on the future makes Israel expect with increasing tension that future which only Yahweh can bring, and which then will be definitive, once for all. Such an expectation has nothing to do with crystal-gazing or an un-veiling of the future. It is rather an insight of faith, gained by the knowledge of God's dealings with his people. Only the unconditional surrender to Yahweh's faithfulness and the living traditions that are related to it can bring any certainty about the future. In terms of man's historicity Yahweh's faith-fulness is expectation of a future, certainty about the goodness of the plan of creation which is both the beginning and the *eschaton*, the ultimate end. It is 'very good' (Gen 1:31). In other words, man's future as seen by God (the bible puts these words into Yahweh's mouth), is 'very good', a future of salva-tion. The lack of salvation, temporary or possibly final, is of man's own doing. It is interesting here that biblical thought about the beginning ('protology') is intertwined with eschatolo-gical thought. This protology, as formulated in the final draft of the creation story in Genesis, can only be understood on the basis of actual experience of God's faithfulness with its consequent eschatological expectations. The story of creation is therefore also an eschatological statement.

V *Eschaton* and future

What, however, is the connection between future and *escha-ton*? O. Procksch, G. von Rad and T. Vriezen[4] rightly main-tain against V. Maag[5] that in the old testament the belief in

God's dominion is not identical with the kingdom of God in the eschatological sense. Moreover, for centuries Israel practised its religion without expecting a hereafter. Apart from the late apocalyptic eschatology in the old testament, expressions such as 'the last days' do not refer to an existence beyond this earth, beyond history, but to a future within this world. The *eschaton* is marked by newness and universalism but it is all in a concept of history which remains on this side of the beyond. To this Ezekiel and Deutero–Isaiah add the idea of an approaching nearness. Throughout the prophetic tradition the picture of God's day of judgement is thrown on to the screen of earthly history; it is the picture of an expectation of a future in this world, this history. Only in Daniel and the very latest apocalyptic insertions into earlier prophetic traditions does the day of Yahweh put a full stop to history. The *eschaton* then refers to a situation beyond this earth, or at least to the time immediately preceding the end of time. But even in the probably late apocalyptic passage in Isaiah 24–7 the last days are still seen within the reality of the history of this world: the old people of God is then given its final eschatological status without mentioning whether history will still go on after that. Not until the book of Daniel is there question of a transcendent eschatology and is there talk of a post-historical existence, expressed in the powerful religious symbol of resurrection. That there will be a future for the historical past, and even for the dead, appears only very late in the old testament.

For centuries, therefore, the belief in Yahweh could be practised meaningfully without the assertion of a transcendent, post-historical and final fulfilment. This development in revelation shows that one does not live religiously for the sake of the hereafter. The development of Israel's faith shows that the unquestionable value of the covenant, the actual relationship between the historic Israel and God, provides the hermeneutic context for a belief in a transcendent eschatology. The 'setting in life' of the eschatological expectation beyond this world is the temporal all-surpassing meaning of the actual relationship with the living God. This conceals the hidden urge towards a transcendent future. For some time devout Israelites had already had some inkling of the idea that even death has no power over him whom God loves. Most powerfully perhaps in Psalms 16, 49 and 73 that spiritual experience of relationship with God is expressed which would sooner or later destroy the idea of the state after death as one of excommunication from life, from life in this world with one's fellows in communion with God, and so pave the way for a transcendent eschatology. In these psalms Yahweh's faithfulness fosters the idea that love must be immortal and definitive, that through this love we know that we are in God's hand not only *in* but also *after* death. Beyond this vague hunch the psalmists had no appropriate terminology to express the certainty of this spiritual experience, and the concept of resurrection provided the first suitable formula.

The present, then, understood as the actual relationship with God and experienced historically as God's dealings with man, is not only the hermeneutic principle for the interpretation of religious expectations of the future, but also the principle which links the future of this earth with the transcendent *eschaton*. The bible gives us no anticipatory historical report on this *eschaton*. We know nothing about the transcendent last things—judgement, Christ's return, heaven, hell, purgatory—except in so far as they are already indicated in the course of historical events expressing the actual relationship between the God of the covenant and mankind, particularly in Christ, 'the last Adam', or 'man of the *eschaton*' (1 Cor 15:45). Eschatology, therefore, does not allow us to withdraw from earthly history, because only in the depth of this history can eternity begin to take shape. The post-terrestrial *eschaton* is but a question of the manner in which what is already growing in the history of this world will receive its final fulfilment. This analysis seems to confirm Rahner's position: 'To speak from the present to the future is eschatology; to speak from the future to the present is apocalyptic.'[6] Eschatology is the expression of the belief that history is in God's hands, that the history of the world can reach its fulfilment in communion with God and that it will be brought to this fulfilment in Christ who embodies God's promise. Eschatology does not allow us to cash in on the hereafter, but it is something to be achieved responsibly by all the faithful within the framework of our terrestrial history. Faced with the real evil existing in history, eschatology expresses the belief that the true faithful can and must bend this history into the salvation of all. This must be done within the perspective of present world history, in newness and in the context of universality. This salvation must already be achieved now in our history, in this world, and so this history becomes itself a prophecy of the final and transcendent *eschaton*. It is the promise of a new world, a powerful symbol which sets us thinking and above all acting. The credibility of this promise lies in the renewal now of our human history. Through their justification the faithful themselves become responsible for the newness of this human world whose dimension in depth will be perpetuated into eternity. For this eternity does not come after our time or our history, but is both the transcendent and the intrinsic ultimate fulfilment of this history itself.

All exegetes accept that the biblical words about the kingdom of God are connected with Jesus' own message. In Jesus the world is given the last promise. But in Jesus of Nazareth we see that the *eschaton* is a post-historical event about which we can only speak from the angle of a history understood in the terms of faith. The raising of Jesus to the status of Lord is a saving act of God which, at a point of time, turned the history which ended in his death into a fulfilled history. That is why it touches our own terrestrial history. We are faced here with a real event which is embedded in history and yet is not historical but eschatological. While the apocalyptic approach puts the *eschaton* at the end of the history of this world, christianity has put it within history itself. Because of the ambiguity of human freedom this history remains open to the future; on the other hand, it already carries the judgement within it. For in the man Jesus the future of mankind has been revealed to us: the fulfilment of the life of Jesus himself, in both its individual and collective-social aspects.

The new world, in Jesus Christ, irrevocably promised and actually on its way, is therefore not a prefabricated reality but is coming into being as an historical process of acting-in-faith in this world. In its present realisation this history is a prophetic pointer to the final fulfilment which can no longer be achieved or expressed in terms of terrestrial history. It does not end this terrestrial history by leaving it behind but by bringing it wholly to its fulfilment. That is why we can only speak haltingly about the final eschatological kingdom and mainly in images and symbols that have grown out of contrast experiences (the 'this-situation-should-be-changed' type) in our still growing world: 'there shall be neither mourning nor crying nor pain any more' (Rev 21 : 4); 'new heavens and a new earth in which righteousness dwells' (2 Peter 3: 13). In the concrete the hermeneutics and exegesis of the final kingdom therefore consist mainly in the stressing of the actual commitment of the faithful to the renewal of this human history of ours. Only this constructive christian activity provides a credible exegesis or interpretation of what we believe when, as the people of God, we confess: 'I believe in eternal life.' In other words, I believe in an earthly, historical life that is truly *life* and that is stronger than death for him who believes in the living God, who gave man the final promise of his faithfulness in Jesus Christ 'for ever and ever' and to the end of time.

The fact that transcendent eschatology arose very late in the history of revelation defends genuine religion against Freudian or marxist criticism which maintains that belief in the hereafter is by definition projection and alienation. The joy of being able to serve Yahweh has made the believer in God's revelation keep silent about the hereafter for centuries in spite of the pressure of opinions that were current in neighbouring cultures. Israel's greatest tragedy was that it had to make up its mind about its ideas of death, in other words, about the experience of the fact that death still snatched this living-with-God away from God's sovereignty (Deut 30: 19–20). But in the end, this living-with-the-living-God on this earth had to yield its secret: such a life makes even death a relative event, it is stronger than death. There is no trace of a natural immortality of the soul in either the old or the new testament. But we do find there the primacy of the actual covenant relationship with the living God who is faithfulness and therefore also future, even for the faithful who have died. The kingdom of Yahweh cannot be reconciled with being dead. In its cultural and religious history Israel had already passed its peak before it realised—in fact, only two centuries before Jesus came—the genuine eschatological implications of its old faith and saw that history, seen as the dealings of God with man through his covenant, contained far more than could be related in a purely historical fashion. In its historicity history is a prophecy which points beyond the historical events to the transcendent *eschaton*. This means that only an analysis of the way the christian lives in this world can tell us something in very sober terms about the great eschatological themes, resurrection, judgment, the *parousia*, the fulfilment of a bodily mankind in full communion with God, in short, about what we call 'heaven', a reality which only man himself can twist into a negation, a self-built hell, the rejection of that love which is the foundation of this total communion.

On the basis of these few hermeneutical principles theology can be seen as the rational and meaningful unfolding of what shows itself in history. It is not the only possible rational interpretation of reality, but it can show that in its affirmation of reality the christian faith gives a humanly meaningful, intelligible and responsible interpretation of man and his world. Thus it can enter into a genuine dialogue with the many other interpretations current in this world—for the good of all.

2
THE CONTEXT AND VALUE OF FAITH-TALK

I Relationship with lived experience as criterion for the meaning of theological interpretations

Insofar as it has any connection with the meaning of the traditional content of faith, the crisis in the churches points clearly enough to the inadequacy of the principle of 'language-meaning from use' which is employed by certain linguistic analysts and which can be briefly defined as the principle that the meaning of language is determined by the language game in which it is used. When a certain language game is accepted, various internal criteria for an intelligible use of language can be defined within it. The crisis of faith in the churches, however, exposes the weakness of this method of verification, which is itself a corrected version of the earlier verification principle. It is, after all, becoming widely recognised that the use of the church's language in the church herself, that is, the community of this 'language game', is no longer understood by those who use this language, the believers themselves. The language game of the church has, in other words, become problematical for the members of the church community. Anyone who has tried to trace the causes of this loss of understanding is bound to come to the conclusion that at least one of these causes is that the language of the church becomes regarded as meaningless as it ceases, in one way or another, to have a recognisable reference to lived experience in the world. However necessary logical and linguistic criteria (see chapter 3) may be for the meaningful use of language within a definite language game, language and linguistic symbols only have meaning in our everyday use of language when they express or conceptualise everyday lived experience. In other words, language only communicates meaning when it expresses an experience that is shared by the community. The most recent form of linguistic analysis[7] is basically in agreement here with the earlier view expressed by Merleau-Ponty, namely that linguistic symbols have meaning on the basis of their relationship with lived experience.[8]

To ask whether this use of language is meaningful or intelligible is therefore to ask two questions. First, what aspect of ordinary human experience, which is shared by everybody or at least by very many people, is expressed in this use of language? Secondly, is it only a question of applying the logical and linguistic rules of this particular language game correctly? The crisis in the church's use of language, in her creeds, liturgy, catechesis and theology, therefore points to the fact that this language can no longer be experienced by many believers as a reflection of their contemporary association with reality. Words such as 'redemption', 'justification', 'resurrection' and 'reconciliation' have, for instance, lost their meaning for many people in the church because they are unable to see any relationship between these key concepts and their lived experience, which is now expressed in other concepts drawn from the familiar sphere of modern socio-political life and interhuman relationships.

However closely the question of meaning may be connected with that about truth, the two questions are different and the question of meaning always precedes that of truth, because only a meaningful statement can be true or false. The inevitable result of this is that, whenever this relationship with human experience is no longer felt, no attention is paid to christians when they begin to speak about redemption, justification, resurrection or reconciliation. This attitude is characteristically put by the expression: 'It means nothing to me', which implies, at a more reflective level, that the speaker cannot immediately see any relationship between the theological statement and his own ordinary experience, with the result that there is no reason to investigate that statement seriously. This may be rather a hasty conclusion, but what should be borne in mind in this context is whether the theological statement was really formulated in such a way that human experience was

in fact expressed in it, and whether it was therefore a challenge to human understanding. The fault may perhaps lie
more with the theological speaker than with the experiencing
listener.

It is therefore necessary to verify systematically every dogmatic and theological statement in a process of what may be
called hermeneutics of experience before embarking on a
system of hermeneutics of christian tradition, because it is not
by any means certain that every real aspect of human experience will be expressed in the self-understanding of christian
experience which, of course, forms an integral part of that experience. If it is correct to call theology the actualising continuation of the christian history of interpretation, then what
is primarily required, especially now that we can no longer
rely on the fact that our listeners will be by birth and upbring-
ing totally catholic, is a critical enquiry into the presuppositions of the fundamental christian option.

What is said about Jesus in the church's interpretation of
faith has therefore, if it is to be meaningful and intelligible to
us—and this is the most important condition to be fulfilled if
we are to give ourselves completely in faith—to have a real
relationship with our ordinary everyday experience with our
fellow-men in the world. If this bond between christian faith
and our experience in the world is broken, christian faith can
no longer be understood by us, and our decision for or against
christianity will no longer be relevant. We shall ignore it, like
all unintelligible things which are so irrelevant that they are
not worth reflecting about. If the church's talk about Jesus
Christ can only be understood, moreover, within the limits
of the church's use of language, that is as a consistent and
coherent whole, by those who use that language within the
church, while it cannot at the same time be made clear that
this language system has any relationship with man's everyday
lived experience, then this talk about Christ will, because it
is unintelligible to non-christians, lose all its power to con-
vince people and bring them into the church. It will also, in
the long run, become a serious problem for the members of
the church as well.

The basic condition, then, for every interpretation of faith
which is faithful to the gospel is the meaningfulness of that
interpretation. In other words, it must reflect real experience.
On the other hand, the experience of our everyday existence

in the world must also give meaning and reality to our theological talk. If this basic condition is not satisfied, in other words, if human experience is not expressed in theological language, then such theological talk is meaningless, and the question whether the new interpretation is either orthodox or heretical is *a priori* superfluous.

I should like to stress that I am not claiming that it is possible to deduce from our human experiences the real christian meaning of, for example, Jesus' resurrection or the redemptive significance of his life. What I am saying, however, is that the christian meaning of the resurrection and of redemption will be *a priori* unintelligible to us and we shall be prevented from attempting to answer questions concerning truth which affect our decision for or against christianity if the universally intelligible content of these concepts does not include human experience. It is only when this is the case that the condition is fulfilled for our being able to confirm the truth of christianity by giving ourselves completely in faith, and for us and others to be able to decide for or against the christian message. The new challenge confronting christianity is not so much the threat of hostility on the part of anti-christians. It is rather the danger that the church will become a completely irrelevant, closed group, a sect that has nothing to offer to others and to which others are therefore indifferent.

In conclusion, we may therefore say that all theological interpretation must, as a reflection about religious talk, have a meaning that can be understood in and by the world. In other words, it must have what Paul van Buren has called a 'secular meaning'. In my opinion, the relationship with lived human experience replaces the criterion of objective verification or falsification which is used by many linguistic analysts, including Paul van Buren himself, with the result that they regard all religious statements either as meaningless or as expressions of a non-cognitive 'blik'. This, however, does not provide us with any criterion for the reactualisation of the christian message as a whole: it only gives us a criterion for the intelligibility of an orthodox—or possibly a heterodox—interpretation.

II The doxological character of theological interpretations

A confession of faith, expressing, at least in outline, at a cer-

tain period of history, the good news of the gospel, has
primarily a doxological value; in other words, it is a confession praising God for everything that he does for us in human
history.[9] If we take as our point of departure the idea of the
first Vatican Council that the 'mutual connection between the
mysteries' is a theological criterion on the basis of which it is
necessary to judge truths which, compared with the essential
message, have to be regarded as peripheral, then these truths
which result from or are presupposed in the christian message,
must have the same doxological meaning, at least so long as
they aim to be not merely logically consistent, but theologically relevant. A theological statement attempts to express the
content of a definite act of trust in God. The dogma of
original sin, for example, is a definition of a thankful confession and of a religious act of surrender to God in Jesus Christ,
of the consciousness that life can and must be different despite
our ethical and religious impotence. Again and again theologians have argued rather meaninglessly about the logical
consistency of less central truths while their doxological meaning has been lost. Whether what has been called *veritas cath-
olica* (by which is meant truth which is not included in the
apostles' creed, but which has nevertheless been given importance in the minds of many believers by historical circumstances and so has become part of catholic belief) is relevant
to faith and theology primarily depends on the special doxological character of such truth, and much less on the fact that it
has been dogmatically defined. A great deal of what theologians say is probably 'logically' true, but it is frequently forgotten that the religious meaning of their statements ought to
be brought to light. What is logically true and consistent does
not always, after all, have a religious meaning, but the theologian is ultimately concerned above all with that religious
significance.

This insight into the doxological meaning of the language
of faith should make us careful when we use certain theological statements. All christians, including theologians and members of the church's teaching office, derive their thought and
speech not only from revelation, but also from all kinds of
conscious and unconscious presupposition. In the light of
cultural and social presuppositions, which are usually not
critically reflected upon, but rather accepted unquestioningly,
theologians and the church's teaching office can therefore draw

a conclusion from the kerygma which is logically consistent, compelling and coherent according to the original presupposition, but which may not be valid if this social and cultural presupposition later appears to be wrong. The logically consistent conclusion then simply becomes superfluous. Within a definite model of interpretation which, even if it is used dogmatically, never imposes itself as a necessity, all kinds of conclusions certainly follow—for example, in the sphere of christology—and these conclusions have to be accepted on pain of heterodoxy within that particular model, although they do not follow within another and equally orthodox model of interpretation and are therefore superfluous. If the doxological value of such a conclusion is not apparent in itself (and as long as the conclusion functions within that model of interpretation, it only shares in the doxological value of the main truth) we are always bound to doubt its theological relevance. That, at least, is my own experience as a theologian.[10]

The doxological character of a theological interpretation can, if it is used sensitively, give a direction to the theological application of criteria for an interpretation that is correct and faithful. These criteria, which will be discussed in greater detail in the following chapter, do not, it is true, provide a ready-made certainty. This kind of certainty is, after all, remote from the certainty of faith, which is ultimately a trust that God's promise is with the church and that the church can, despite human failings, never entirely disappoint God because of the gift of creative penitence that she has received. There are, however, certain unmistakable criteria which have to be satisfied if full respect is to be paid to the demands of reason, which again is a gift of God, and therefore also to the structures within which God's grace and help is effectively present in his church. The church is doubtless faithful to the Son's message because of the charism of the Holy Spirit, not because of any divine intervention, without leaving traces of believing creativity at the level of the history of the church.[11] I should like now to follow up these traces of believing creativity, leaving it entirely to God, and to the unarmed and indeed disarming mystery of faith in God, how he fulfils his promise of faithfulness to his church throughout the centuries, in and through man's imperfection.

3
LINGUISTIC CRITERIA

From the very beginning of christianity the problem of theological hermeneutics has been connected essentially with the
bible. On the one hand, christianity is an interpretation of
previous literature, in this case the old testament, a *hermeneia*
of the law, the writings and the prophets from the point of
view of the hermeneutical situating of the event of Jesus in
the light of his resurrection. On the other hand, christianity
is not simply the christian interpretation of the old testament
—this interpretation has itself been set down in writing in the
literature of the new testament. This in turn calls for interpretation, so that our contemporary interpretation of the
bible is an interpretation of an interpretation.

In both cases, however, as in every case of literary interpretation, it is not simply a question of interpreting a text.
Interpreting the old testament is interpreting a reality and a
history in the light of faith in Yahweh. It is, in other words,
a Yahwistic interpretation of history. The old testament is
therefore the central literary instrument of interpretation of
the Jewish people as the people of God. The new testament
is also the central literary instrument of the christian interpretation of Jesus' life and death, seen in the light of his resurrection and within an old testament sphere of understanding.
In this way, a believers' interpretation of reality is presented
in literary documents. What we have is a reality to be interpreted, but this is done via a literature that itself has to be
interpreted. Christianity cannot be reduced to a religion of the
word or the book, but the mediation of what is expressed in

language and in writing cannot be ignored when one thinks of christianity. On the one hand, theology is confronted with the hermeneutic problem as this appears in the study of literature and, on the other, christianity is a belief-interpretation of a reality and of history. On this basis, theological hermeneutics are clearly confronted with the hermeneutics of history and with the hermeneutics of philosophy's attempts to analyse and define reality.

This brief introduction shows that theological hermeneutics, as practised by theologians such as Rudolf Bultmann, Ernst Fuchs and Gerhard Ebeling and as set out in their formal structures by Hans Georg Gadamer, are essentially phenomenological, leaving the reality of the event of Jesus, interpreted as an act of God in Jesus, outside the sphere of criticism. Karl Barth, Bultmann, and those who have followed them act in this as convinced believers, presupposing the reality of the interpreted event of Jesus as a safe area at the frontier of which critical hermeneutics must halt. It is only within this presupposition that a search is made for hermeneutic rules which will be able to express the same thing in a way which is different, translated or interpreted, not reduced, faithful to the gospel and yet contemporary. Hermeneutics of this kind are justified and they are, in the first instance, also sufficient.

There is, however, another and more fundamental problem which is purely hermeneutic—the interpretation of the human event of Jesus, insofar as this is God's act of revelation in history or in the *kerygma*. *Hermeneia* at this level is regarded by many scholars as both justified and urgently required at present. There is an abundance of interpretation of the event of Jesus which is not christian: a Jewish interpretation, an atheistic, purely secular interpretation as well as other non-western and non-christian religious and non-religious interpretations of all kinds. On the basis of all these data, theologians are bound to conduct a hermeneutic investigation of this presupposition of christian theology, which up to now has been accepted without question. This fundamental investigation has been attempted by Wolfhart Pannenberg, although it must be admitted that he has not carried it through in an entirely satisfactory way. He has, however, gone deeper into the whole question of theological hermeneutics than Bultmann and his followers. He has extended the *hermeneia* to include the hitherto unquestioningly accepted presuppositions of dialectical theology (that of Barth and later of Bultmann and his followers) and of the whole of catholic theology.[12] In other words, Pannenberg has not restricted hermeneutics to a theological interpretation of the bible, in which the word of God is accepted simply on the authority of the bible itself and on the basis of biblical inspiration. He has gone much further back, into the interpretation of history itself, to which scripture bears witness. The concept of an external authority, of scripture or of the church's teaching office, plays no part in Pannenberg's programme of fundamental research; what is involved is the inner authority of the event itself which, because of its meaning, understood by us, demands our understanding and our adhesion.

Presupposing a basis of historical and critical hermeneutics, I should like to throw a little light on a number of requirements for a system of theological hermeneutics, dealing with them in order of increasing importance. Theology interprets God's word, but this is expressed in human words. Theology, as the hermeneutics of God's word, is therefore also concerned with semantics: it presupposes a concept of what language is. The theologian must therefore listen very carefully to those who have specialised in the study of language and have considered language from different points of view. This approach is based on a respect for the word of God, which, although it is only spoken and recognised in human words, cannot be confused with man's own inventions or imaginings. The theologian has therefore to concern himself with structuralist linguistics and with logical linguistic analysis and must study these not as philosophies, but rather as sciences. He must also carefully consider the phenomenological philosophy of language.

On the other hand, the theologian is above all concerned with the interpretation of a reality which is expressed through literary documents. He will therefore have to pay close attention to an ontology of language which analyses the expression of reality in human language and views human speech in its ontological dimension, that is, as the universal revelation of being in the word. Christianity is not gnosticism, however, or a theoretical doctrine of salvation, and the original confession of christian faith was therefore the theoretical aspect of the sacramental praxis of christian life (the creed used at baptism).

For these reasons we are bound to point out how insufficient any purely theoretical hermeneutics are, and how orthopraxis forms an essential part of any criterion used for verification in a credible interpretation of faith.

The divisions in this chapter ought therefore to be clear. The aim of the chapter itself is to provide clear information in a convenient form. I shall in each case outline the basic principles of the linguistic approach that is most relevant to theology before going on to show how this approach can be applied to theological hermeneutics.

I Structuralism or structural linguistic analysis[13]

The theoretical model of the new 'structuralist' linguistic analysis is based on what is known as a structural reduction. The fundamental postulate of structuralism is that the matter discussed and the subjects speaking are bracketed off from one another. There is therefore a sharp distinction between language as an institution ('language', *la langue, die Sprache*) and language as a linguistic and verbal event ('speech', 'talk', or 'discourse'; *la parole, le discours; die Rede*).

Structuralism is a study of language simply as an institution, that is, as a structure independent of the subject who is speaking, and of which the individual may even be unconscious. It can be illustrated from chess: language as a structure is like the state of the game at a given moment, whereas language as a verbal event is like a new move which changes the state of affairs. In structuralism, language is regarded as an autonomous, closed system of signs, with the inevitable consequence that its semantics have to be analysed synchronistically, according to the structure of language at a given moment, not diachronistically, according to the course of its development.

The history of a word often has very little to tell us about that word's contemporary meaning. Apart from the history of language, there is also the structure of language, consisting of laws of balance which have repercussions on the elements of language and which, at every moment of history, are dependent on synchrony. The linguistic structures are not sought in the terms themselves, but in a system of relationships between the terms. Language is therefore above all a system of relationships in which a word or a term has no meaning of its own apart from being a sign which is distinguished, within the linguistic system, from all other linguistic signs. In other words, as a sign, the term or word is a distinctive element in a lexical system which, when other elements change, itself changes too. Each sign only has value in conjunctive or disjunctive relationship with the other signs. The whole complex of meanings thus forms a system on the basis of distinctions and oppositions.

The laws of balance affecting the system, in other words the self-regulation of the system, are relatively independent of its laws of development, with the result that semantics are primarily governed synchronistically, while diachrony occurs only in comparison between two synchronistic systems separated from each other in time. It must, of course, be borne in mind here that language is permanently in motion, so that in reality diachrony intervenes in the synchrony.

According to structuralism, there are no external relationships in the linguistic system; in a dictionary, for example, one word points to another word, never to a thing. All factors outside language are ignored and only the characteristics within the closed linguistic and semantic system are taken into account.

This purely structural approach clearly excludes any possibility of hermeneutics. Within this linguistic theory, there are only elements that can be classified according to certain rules. On this basis, structures or systems are presented and their function has to be analysed, although no light is thrown on them from the self-understanding subject. The ultimate aim of structuralism is therefore a new objectivity, quite independent of such a subject. The positive element of this is the structural function—the syntactical and lexical functions ensure the semantic function of the words and their combinations.

This structural linguistic theory is only indirectly connected with theological hermeneutics. Because of its structural reduction, it excludes precisely that with which the theologian is really concerned, the offer of a meaning, the significant content of a message which is directed towards the subject. What is more, the theologian is concerned above all with history and therefore with diachrony, that is with the question how a message originally formulated twenty centuries ago for people of that time can appeal to and have meaning for people of today.

On the other hand, however, the theologian cannot ignore

the contribution made by structuralism in his hermeneutic approach to the bible. Both dualism and monism are out of place in the philosophy of man. There is no authentically human realm of freedom in man *alongside* a determined zone of functionality. Although humanity cannot be reduced to pure functionality, the whole of human existence is permeated with this functional aspect. Freedom and functionality are closely interwoven. A distinctive attribute of humanity is that there is subjectivity in man's objectivity and objectivity in his subjectivity. In this connection, however, it is important to bear in mind that human freedom is not something that is merely 'given'. It is rather something that has to be realised, something in which it is possible to fail or which, because of various factors, is simply not realised.

We may go further and say that even the human phenomenon known as speech has independent structures which lead their own life. These structures are, of course, scientifically investigated by those who translate the theory of structuralism into practice. We may therefore say that a few minimal demands are made by the structuralists and these have to be satisfied by theology before real hermeneutics of the bible and the church's teaching office can be properly practised. A structural and primarily synchronistic analysis of the key words contained in the bible has thus to precede theological hermeneutics. Expressed in another way, the condition of theological hermeneutics is structural analysis.

In theology, the exegesis of God's word expressed in human words, it is certainly a question of understanding the meaning of the biblical message. If, however, these words are to have any meaning for the one who hears or reads them, they must form part of a structure which, at least negatively, co-determines the meaning of what is said. Only the contextual structure sifts the multiplicity of meanings contained in the words, by which what is said can be meaningfully recognised and interpreted. Structuralism emphasises the possibility that these words may have many different meanings, but at the same time insists that not all of these various meanings have to be present in every context, or in fact are present. If this is overlooked, words tend to be isolated from their syntax, with the consequence that contextual meanings are made independent and raised to the level of universal concepts and used to support a theology of the old or new testaments.

In the first place, then, key-words in the bible such as God, sin and grace, the covenant, love, justice and so on should be studied synchronistically. Without giving rise to misunderstanding it is impossible to set out under one general key-word the many different meanings, for example, of the word *hesed* —love, mercy, etc.—at various periods in the old testament. (Despite certain praiseworthy exceptions, this certainly often happens in Kittel's well-known work.) In his criticism of biblical dictionaries, James Barr has said correctly, I think, although perhaps with a certain exaggeration, that most semantic studies and dictionaries of the bible do not satisfy even the most minimal demands of structural linguistic analysis.

This can lead to various forms of ideology. It is possible, for example, to conclude from an analysis of Hebrew which does not penetrate to the deepest level of grammar that there is a difference between the Semitic and the Greek mind and this is to a very great extent an ideological distinction. If rigorous structural analysis is neglected, the synthetic method may lead to a kind of history of ideas and not to a genuinely linguistic analysis of the use of words in the bible, which is the indispensable prerequisite for any biblical theology. This confusion of theological realities and linguistic phenomena easily produces quite unjustified generalisations. The structuralists, who do not claim that their structural study of language is a linguistic philosophy, admit, of course, that speech also has reference, has something to say about things, but the investigation of this is quite a different task which, as such, does not form part of the question of the correct use of language.

We may therefore conclude that structuralism can help us to expose many prejudices and, even more important, many unjustified generalisations in theological hermeneutics, which should favour a purer form of hermeneutics. The hermeneutical method should therefore be combined with the structural method. In isolation, each method tends to come to a dead end. There is therefore no question here of a choice between one and the other, as many critics claim.

II Phenomenological linguistic analysis[14]
The phenomenological approach to language also begins with a reduction; in this case, judgment about reality is suspended and that reality is, as it were, placed in brackets. In itself, this

reduction has no metaphysical claims. All that is involved is the structure of the phenomenon as such.

The phenomenology of language attempts to throw light on the relationship between language as a system of signs and the verbal event as an intentionality. In other words, it tries to answer the question, how is language as an institution used in a meaningful verbal event? Language is therefore not thought of in isolation, but is seen in its mediating function as an offer of meaning (its referential and representative aspect) as self-expression and as communication. Speaking is above all saying something about something, or about someone, to someone. These three aspects of language are not studied in structural linguistic analysis. In phenomenological linguistic analysis, moreover, meaning is conceived as the ability to understand signs as referring to reality, that is, in the purely phenomenological sense, as the correlative of consciousness or experience. Speech therefore means bringing something to light. The intentionality of speech presupposes that speech is directed towards something. One says something ('meaning') about an object ('reference'). The phenomenology of language thus goes a step further than structural linguistic analysis, in that the linguistic unit analysed by phenomenology is the sentence or phrase. 'In examining the sentence, we leave the sphere of language as a system of signs and enter another realm, that of language as an instrument of communication, the expression of which is the discourse.'[15] Whereas the word is regarded in structural linguistic analysis as a differential element in a lexical system, in the phenomenological study of language it is seen as a function in a phrase, with the result that it participates in the whole phrase and comes to signify reality. The verbal event or the use of language makes history within language as an institution which comes to bear what Paul Ricoeur has called the 'scars' of usage, with the consequence that it returns, with the cumulative enrichment that comes from its being used, to the dictionary, which therefore has to be edited and adapted again and again. In this way, the system enters the diachrony of history.

From the phenomenological point of view, then, speech always has a triadic structure,[16] which has been called the 'discourse situation' by John MacQuarrie,[17] in other words, the language situation as a human phenomenon. Represented in the form of a diagram, language as an institution is at the centre of a triangle, mediating between the subject speaking, the listeners or readers, and the content of the conversation. The whole, the language situation, is the verbal event in which meaning becomes clear. Any discussion about the meaning of a text or of speech has therefore to take this triadic whole of the language situation into account. Dissociated from this situation, language is simply an abstraction and the interpretation of a text is not a responsible undertaking. Because of the tension between language as an institution and language as a verbal event, the understanding of texts and of speech is only possible in the act of re-interpretation. The minimal requirement of this act of interpretation is structural analysis, but the whole language situation has above all to be analysed. It is important in this context to throw some light on each of the three aspects of the language situation.

In saying something, the subject speaking also expresses himself as a being in the world. This reflects the existential aspect of the linguistic event, 'existential' here referring to the existence of man in general, in his environment and together with his world, not in the narrower sense of individual existence. This self-expression includes a range of possibilities, from expression related to the whole of reality, especially in religious statements, to the expression of objective knowledge or science in which the existential factor is on the verge of disappearing, although it never disappears entirely.

In addition to self-expression, there is the referential and representational aspect of language, as conveying a meaning, in its function of saying something about something. Leaving aside meta-language (a statement about a statement) speech always transcends itself by its reference to elements outside language which co-determine its use. Apparently under the influence of such extra-linguistic factors, for example, the Eskimos have some thirty different words for snow.

Finally, there is the aspect of communication. The person listening to the subject who is speaking or who reads that subject's text is also acting as a being in the world. Communication therefore only takes place in the act of re-interpretation and, as a passing on of what is said, is always defective if the partners do not share the same presuppositions and the same sphere of understanding. It is therefore essential that the presuppositions of the subject who speaks or writes and those of the interpreter should be analysed so as to make the offer by the subject of a definite meaning accessible to the person who is listening or reading and to prevent breakdowns in communication. In this, I would agree with Dilthey and Gadamer[18] that a merging together of various spheres takes place here, with a resulting understanding and communication in a communal sense.

This phenomenological approach to language, in which the whole language situation is analysed in its triadic structure of meaning, self-expression and communication is, of course, much more directly connected with the theological interpretation of faith than structuralism is. This applies especially to the aspect of communication: the offer of meaning by the subject who speaks or writes the text can only be made personally in the act of re-interpretation. In this sense, theological interpretation is the translation or transformation of one way of speaking theologically, mythical religious speech for instance, into a different way of speaking theologically, such as existential religious speech or existential interpretation of mythological speech. In this transformation there is no intention to misunderstand the first way of speaking. (It is possible that the myth may contain some remnant which cannot be interpreted purely existentially and which also requires an ontological interpretation.) The language of theological interpretation can, by definition, because it is a statement about a statement, be called a meta-language. It has to respect the intentionality of the language of the bible or of the church's teaching office, but it must also be able, as a meta-language, to express in a suitable way the intentionality of the bible. (A purely empirical language, for example, cannot do this suitably.) This is why a critical investigation of the key biblical words and their context is necessary in any theological interpretation of the bible, first of all according to the minimal demands of structural linguistic analysis and then according to the phenomenological approach, which will take the whole contextual structure into account. This critical examination has also to include a further analysis of the meta-language in which the message of the bible is interpreted.

This theological interpretation can, because it includes not only its own presuppositions, but also a previously evaluated view of man and the world (the aspect of self-expression), bring about an alienation from the content of the language to be interpreted. If it is to be successful, then, it must include a critical analysis of the meta-language in which the christian message is translated. Theological hermeneutics thus imply a critical investigation of its own sphere of understanding, which can only be interpreted effectively if the past, with its constantly changing spheres of understanding, is analysed. That is why theological hermeneutics cannot be practised without the contribution made by the history of ideas and by philosophy, insofar as these are concerned with the changing spheres of understanding in which repeated attempts have been made by christians to interpret the christian message. It is only if this condition is satisfied that communication will be made possible in the act of re-interpretation.

Unlike a simple repetition of the christian message which is purely material and therefore unintelligible in a changed sphere of understanding, justified theological hermeneutics are characterised by the fact that our contemporary experiences and ways of thinking play an essential part in our rendering of the text to be understood. At the same time, however, the intention in theological hermeneutics is always to preserve the christian message entire, however differently it may be expressed.

In this phenomenological approach, any subtle manipulation of the distinction between the essential core and the changing form in which that essence is clothed is made ambiguous for the theologian, although it is not made simply absurd. It is in any case impossible to separate the lasting essence from its temporal form—a contemporary interpretation is, in the end, only another interpretation. If we attempt to separate the lasting element, we inevitably run the risk of declaring timeless an element that is restricted to a particular time. What is lasting—the identity itself—is, however, only given in what is temporally relevant, in non-identity. The word of God, which is only given to us in the historical form of human words, the language of human experience, calls for what Barth and Bultmann correctly called relevant hermeneutics. This interpretation must be intelligible, accessible and, as the christian message, relevant to our own time. It therefore calls, because of the change that has taken place in our presuppositions, for a re-interpretation.

We may therefore summarise the relevance of phenomenological hermeneutic principles to a theological interpretation under three heads. In the first place, there is a need for a critically analysed pre-understanding in any interpretation of the bible. The whole complex of analysed presuppositions, which Heidegger has in my opinion, correctly called the 'hermeneutic situation'[19] implies, at least theoretically, no prior decision about what the bible has to say to us, although it does throw light on the conditions of understanding under which contemporary communication with the christian message is made possible. In this sense the past, scripture and the interpretation of the message throughout the centuries, is interpreted in the light of the present.

In the second place, the movement of this process of interpretation is circular. Our point of departure is a definite pre-understanding, but our intention is to gain a new understanding. The meaning of the text has a reaction on our presuppositions, with the result that they are enlarged, changed or corrected. In this sense theological interpretation is at the same time critical self-interpretation.

In the third place, theological re-interpretation is only possible if the interpreter has other ways of speaking at his disposal. A believer who still lives entirely in a mythological world, for example, cannot interpret myths for us, even though one myth partly demythologises another myth. (The second, earlier, account of creation in Genesis can be compared, for instance, with the first though later creation story.) Re-interpretation is moreover necessary if the way of speaking in which the christian message is presented to us has become a mode of expression which is alien to us and which we cannot verify in our own experience. The most obvious example of this is, again, the mythological way of speaking. Just as pluralism in the interpretation of faith is diachronistically a fact, so too we must accept synchronistic pluralism in contemporary interpretations of faith which are nonetheless faithful to the gospel, although a number of criteria have to be borne in mind (see chapter 4).

Because this theological interpretation contains so many scientific elements, such as the structural analysis of biblical language, textual criticism, philosophy, historical and critical analysis and phenomenological hermeneutics, it must be called 'scientific'. At the same time, however, even though all these scientific elements are postulated, theological hermeneutics must also be called 'an art'. An essential part is played in it

by creative art, which cannot be tied down to rules. This combination of science and art leads to an ethically justified and
responsible interpretation.

Although the triadic structure is common to all verbal
events, special theologically biased phenomenological principles of hermeneutics have resulted from the triadic structure
of this specifically religious language situation. The existential
aspect which characterises all verbal events, the aspect of self-
expression, is much deeper in the case of a religious language
situation, since what is expressed in such a situation is total
existence.[20]

Theological interpretation of the bible is therefore also an
existential interpretation of the bible, although this does not
necessarily mean that the intentionality of the bible is re-
tained, at least in full. Whatever this full intentionality may
be, however, a theological interpretation that is not at the
same time an existential interpretation deserves to be dis-
qualified from the very outset as unfaithful and unbiblical.
(In this, I am using the term 'existential' in the sense of man
living in the world together with his fellow-men in a social
system.)

Because of the distinctively religious character that the language situation has with regard to communication, the
hermeneutic principle is also specified in this respect—the self-
interpretation that is expressed in christian faith is the self-
understanding of a christian community. The hermeneutic
bearer or subject of a theological interpretation is the christian
community, the church as an interpreting community. In one
form or another, then, the reception of a new interpretation
of faith by the christian community is a factor by which a
theological interpretation that is faithful to the gospel can be
known and recognised.

As far as the offered meaning is concerned, in view of the
special nature of the religious language situation, it would
appear that purely phenomenologically orientated hermeneutics based on a phenomenological reduction would be useful,
but certainly insufficient. This type of hermeneutics can show
that theological speech is always an indirect, evocative speech,
even though it may be assertive, but the principle of reduction
prevents this method from helping us to interpret the reality
of what is offered as truth in the biblical message.

III Logical linguistic analysis

It is possible to ask whether logical linguistic analysis or even analytical philosophy can really help to solve the problem of the meaning offered in the gospel. By analytical philosophy, I do not mean one which regards all supra-empirical realities as meaningless, which does often happen, but rather a philosophy which is based on logical linguistic analysis and has, from this basis, developed techniques by which the meaningfulness or meaninglessness of theological questions and answers can be verified.[21]

The first and most important question in logical linguistic analysis is not that of understanding and interpreting the text, but whether the meaningfulness of the text to be interpreted is accepted *a priori*. The latter is not accepted *a priori* in logical analysis. It has to be proved. As soon as the meaningfulness of the text has been established, interpretation within this accepted meaningfulness is no longer a problem according to logical analysis. The first question that is asked by logical analysis is always the critical question of meaning, and this question is asked in such a way as to establish no valid limit *a priori* to the possible meaning of any proposition. If this means that nothing meaningful can be said unless the logical law $p \equiv \sim(\sim p)$ is accepted, then this is self-evident, for every meaningful proposition must respect the logical law of non-contradiction. Logical laws have universal validity, subject to two important conditions, that the period and the point of view of the proposition are not changed. Logical analysis, which is both objective and objectively orientated, is becoming increasingly conscious of the need to take into account the perspectives of time and space from which the subject who speaks or writes a text says something to us. In its logically and universally valid application, logical analysis really takes into account the points of view from which someone says something to us about something. Since A. Tarski in particular, logical analysts have become increasingly aware of the relativity of a closed logical system and of the fact that logical thought is not a timeless network that can be stretched above the empirical and changing world.

For some time now, however, there has been general agreement that there is a difference between logical and linguistic structures. It has been established both ontogenetically, that is in the growth of the individual child, and phylogenetically, that is in the so-called intelligence of higher, though non-linguistic species of apes, that sensory and motory intelligence includes a number of structures which are linked to the general co-ordination of the living being and which cannot be attributed to language and speaking. There is a common opinion that language comes from an already partially structured intelligence and that it in turn imparts a further structure to that intelligence. There are therefore two clearly differentiated but mutually interacting structures—the linguistic and the logical structure. It has furthermore been established that, even before the logical structures can be formed either verbally or linguistically, logical structures are revealed in the actions of the growing child who is not yet able to speak. It is clear, then, that language is not the source of logic, as the neo-positivists tended to claim, but that language is itself based on logic. What has not yet been sufficiently elucidated, however, is the mutual interaction of logical and linguistic structures, especially in the case of the growth of the child. We are, however, justified in regarding the basic convictions of logical positivism and especially the claim that logic is traceable to the linguistic element as no longer tenable.

The proposition that is applied by logical linguistic analysis to all theological interpretation is that, before the question of truth can be posed meaningfully, the question of meaning has to be put, in other words: is the theological problem meaningful or meaningless? This question about meaning and our understanding of it can, according to logical analysis, only be answered in such a way that the question of the criteria for that meaning and consequently for our understanding of that meaning is answered at the same time in any given case.

Logical analysis, then, insists on the fundamental distinction between 'untrue' and 'meaningless'. Propositions can be meaningful or meaningless, but only meaningful propositions can be true or untrue. Meaningless statements, on the other hand, are neither true nor untrue. This is the unmistakable, although of course obvious contribution made by logical analysis, enabling many philosophical or theological problems to be set aside at the very outset as pseudo-problems. In this, however, it should not be forgotten that pseudo-problems have often played an irreplaceable and positive part in the meaningful interpretation of reality. Just as a methodological reduction is involved both in structural and in pheno-

menological linguistic analysis, so too is the point of departure
for logical linguistic analysis a reduction which by-passes the
content and confines itself to logical, formal and structural
rules. The first and most important question is that of the
agreement of thought or speaking with itself: the aim is to
have logically verifiable structures in view. This form of linguistic analysis can therefore be of assistance in theological
hermeneutics.

Like structural linguistic analysis, logical linguistic analysis
also has a less direct link with theological hermeneutics. Some
christians may hesitate to approach the christian message with
logic, although it must be recognised that the connection between human experience and what man believes is also a
logical connection, although of a very special kind. What is
more, religious and theological statements are neither a-logical
nor supra-logical, nor does theology transcend logic. Even the
theologian cannot, within one and the same point of view in
time and space, at the same time affirm and deny something.
If, for example, he says that the believer is *simul iustus et
peccator*, at the same time sinful and justified, he cannot, whatever theological meaning he gives to this, maintain this double
statement within the same point of view.

Apart from this universally valid logic, every language game
also has its own internal logic which has to be judged according to the inner logical criteria of the language game itself.
Logical linguistic analysis therefore obliges the theologian to
formulate much more clearly the context in which religious
language arises and the logical status of religious statements
and theological arguments. It points above all to the basic
logic of religious and theological speech, to what are called its
'disclosure situations'. The situation forming the context of
religious speech is religious life itself or, more generally, the
consciousness of the quest for meaning in man's life in the
world.

In this sense, religious speech always has a secular context
in which the believer is aware of a deeper dimension which
calls for a personal response or else appeals to man's total
existence. Religious language therefore takes ordinary human
language as its model and qualifies this in an appropriate way
so as to evoke a characteristically religious situation. This interpretative experience makes talk about God logically an

indirect way of speaking—an evocative, symbolic, analogous, paradoxical manner of speaking in parables or in models. All talk about God is therefore characterised by the fact that the believer approaches him as the one who transcends everything that can be observed and is yet closely connected with it, as the one who is experienced as incapable of being directly experienced. This is also the logical status of theology: reflective speech in the light of this distinctive experience. As the basic logic of all religious speech, the religious situation is characterised by a subjective transcendence—total commitment on the basis of a special discernment—as the answer to an objective transcendence.[22] We should also note in passing that, in logical and phenomenological linguistic analysis, what is not considered is whether a transcendent reality is in fact disclosed here or whether this is merely experienced by the believer.

Logical linguistic analysis thus throws light on the logical status of theological objectivity, which is different, for example, from the status of historical objectivity in the study of history or from physical objectivity in the study of physics. This form of linguistic analysis also frequently exposes apparently profound but in fact, from the point of view of linguistic analysis, careless ways in which language is used. An example of this is when two expressions, such as 'Jesus has died' and 'Jesus has risen', which have exactly or almost exactly the same grammatical structure, but reflect radically different logical structures, are nevertheless used theologically as equivalents.

In other words, the theologian who is aware of the contribution made by logical analysis will always give an account of what he is saying. 'How do you know?' is a question that he will bear constantly in mind. As soon as we realise that the truth of revelation has not simply come to us out of the blue but that it is expressed as man's interpretation in faith, with the result that revelation is fundamentally God's word in human words; as soon as we understand that revelation is the experience and the expression of what God does in human history; we can regard the truths of faith formally as human language and therefore go on to judge them according to their humanly intelligible meaning. In this, logical linguistic analysis clearly has a part to play, although it cannot provide us with any answer to the question of truth. It can, however, help to answer the question of meaning, since only a meaningful proposition can be true or false. Most linguistic analysts have now passed through the period of neo-positivism and have come to accept that the proposition that human statements are either descriptive or emotive is over-simple. The situational context presents us with a number of different and logically justified ways of speaking. In a word, logical linguistic analysis is beginning to give careful consideration to what was called the language situation in the preceding section.

The philosophy of analysis, then, has no direct contribution to make to the hermeneutical problem, because it stands as it were on the threshold of hermeneutics and is only concerned with the logical epiphenomenon of interpretative speech, as of all speech. All the same, it can be of inestimable assistance to us in our attempts to answer the question of meaning in theology and in our correct use of theological language. If, for example, it can in this way be established that the question itself is not meaningful, then pseudo-problems can be eliminated in advance in theology. If the question is not meaningful, the theological search for an answer is also not meaningful.

The methodically inadequate but meaningful forms of linguistic analysis which we have so far discussed point clearly in the direction of the language game of the whole of human history, the historical dialogue of mankind. In our examination of this, we shall have to consider the possible ontological basis of the phenomenological 'triadic structure' of the language situation to which some logical linguistic analysts give their assent.

IV The ontological aspect of language

We have seen that three forms of linguistic analysis, structuralist and phenomenological and logical analysis, are undeniably useful in our quest for a theologically meaningful interpretation, but that they all begin with a methodological reduction, that is, they place the reality of what is meaningfully said between brackets. We must therefore have recourse to a form of linguistic analysis in which reality itself is brought in. In this context, it is important for the theologian to consider very carefully what Heidegger had to say in his later writings about the ontological aspect of language.[23]

This ontological aspect of language precedes not only the structures of language as analysed by structuralism and logical linguistic analysis, but also the intention of the subjects speaking, as analysed by phenomenological linguistic analysis. The verbal event is seen as the place of dialectical tension between what is manifested and what we express, in our speech, of that manifestation, between the openness of being and our seizing hold of and understanding that being. It is in this place that the priority of the language that addresses us and the language that claims our speaking is manifested.

Our primary and basic relationship with language is therefore not speaking, but listening. The act of speaking cannot be reduced to the structure of linguistic elements or to the subjective intention of the subjects speaking. Heidegger has defined the act of speaking as a mode of being in which being is so constituted that it can be said or expressed. Being causes us to think. In Heidegger's philosophy, the 'linguistic event' is identical with the 'ontological difference', that is, the distinction between being and beings, in which being is not *a* being, but the ground or *logos* of beings. This ontological difference is an event of being itself, an act which allows the being to move into the foreground, which throws light on the being. What is above all remarkable is that there is something rather than nothing and that this appears to us charged with meaning and demanding to be expressed. This presupposes the possibility of appearing, of thinking and of speaking and this possibility is man. Being there (human existence) lets truth as unconcealment happen: 'being man is speaking'. Man exists therefore in the mode of understanding. Language promises us the essence of things. The address of being and man's expression of it together form language. Within speaking, things appear. Language protects being. In the verbal event, being comes to us. Speaking is obedience, a word and answer to the 'silent language of being'.

Language, as Gerhard Ebeling and Ernst Fuchs have correctly deduced from Heidegger's teaching, has itself a hermeneutic function. Something else is echoed in every interpersonal conversation—what is not said and what cannot be said. Speaking is subject to the power of something other than the person speaking—our speaking is guided and determined. It is commanded. There can be no speaking without man who thinks and speaks, but this speaking is still receiving. The essence of language is that it lets beings appear in being. This is why Heidegger said again and again that our present interpretation has to show what is not in the text, but what is nonetheless said. The essence or being of language is the 'language of being', the linguistic expression of being to us. Language is therefore essentially a medium of revelation. Man is not the master, but the shepherd, the 'protector of being'. Speaking is a 'homology'. Speaking thought is determined by the truth of being and this enables man to share in the event of truth.

What is manifested thus passes through the filter of human language. Speech is therefore being subject to the openness of being, and at the same time the responsibility of man who is speaking and who thus protects being in its openness. Speech enables things to enter the sphere of openness and of revelation, towards which man exercises his responsibility as the subject who speaks. The foundation of human responsibility is therefore the universal revelation of being. Language is a revelation of being in the word, the source of all further humanisation.

This ontology of language has clear consequences for theological hermeneutics. There can be no meaningful understanding of christian revelation without a pre-understanding of the real datum that man lives, in his speech, from a 'revelation'. Christian revelation presupposes a sphere of understanding, an explicit or implicit understanding of what the manifestation of being in the word really means. The ontological aspect of language is therefore at least implicitly the prior condition for a christian pre-understanding. This view provides, I believe, Bultmann's purely existential interpretation of the bible with a new perspective and to some extent corrects it, in that it is an existential and ontological understanding of the bible. It is in my opinion most significant and of great importance for our understanding and interpretation of the bible and of faith that being demands to be expressed. On the other hand, however, it should not be forgotten that the universal revelation of being is not the christian revelation.

Man, as created by God, is a being who exists in the mode of self-understanding and the interpretation of reality. God's *logos* is expressed in man's self-understanding. Man's activity *is* God's activity. There is one act in two subjects. It is, of course, true to say that this self-expression is not so profound and so central in all of man's acts: there are everyday acts and specially privileged acts, in which man's 'I in the world' and in society is more committed, with the result that his interpre-

tation of reality is more clearly shown as a sign. If God is also
made intelligible in man's self-interpretation as created by
God, then there may be privileged acts in the creature expressing God's activity in a privileged way—acts which are really
a sign of him as God.

Privileged historical events are, I believe, human events in
which man expresses the ultimate meaning of his existence in
word and deed. It is possible for all human speaking and activity to become God's activity in a privileged sense, just as it
is also possible for the opposite to happen. God's *logos* may
not be expressed in man's understanding of himself or may be
only fragmentarily expressed. (This accounts for religious
pluralism.) Every human event expresses God's being and activity in and through man's being as a creature. All religions
are therefore an answer to something older and more original
than they are.

God's activity in history therefore means, in an interpretation that is both christian and secular, that there are certain
human words and actions in which the characteristic activity
of God, as the creator and redeemer, is revealed in a very
special way. If the historical life of Jesus of Nazareth is God's
decisive act in human history, as christianity claims, then this
is only meaningfully intelligible if the ultimate truth concerning man's life is revealed and realised in an exemplary and
normative way in the human life of Jesus, in contrast to all
other historical events. God's decisive act in human history
must therefore be a unique culminating point in a series of
revelations, the final revelation. It is clear that if an event can
be called a decisive and definitive act of God in history, it can
only function by being received or understood by someone or
by a group. This event has to be understood as having this
decisive power of revelation. Revelation is a revelation of
someone who makes something known and understood by
someone who is able to understand the meaning of it. In other
words, revelation and interpretation are correlative, and no
historical event can be a decisive act of God for us unless we
accept and understand it as something that determines our
understanding of ourselves and of reality. A historical event
is only a decisive act of God in history if and insofar as man's
expressed understanding of himself can be effective as a true
or authentic understanding of his existence. It notifies us, in

other words, that life which is truly human has to be lived in this way.

Christianity teaches that Jesus is that decisive event in human history and that man's particular self-understanding which is in fact the ultimate truth of his life as confronted by God in the world is brought forward in Jesus' person, words and acts.[24]

The believer recognises in Jesus' human life that the whole meaning of man's life consists of God's transcendent love as the only basis of an authentic human life. The believer acknowledges the authority of scripture not so much on the basis of its inspiration—this is an *a posteriori* interpretation, a reflective affirmation of the second order—but rather on the basis of the authentic witness that it bears to an event and its meaning, and because he understands that event as normative.

For the believer, Jesus is the revelation of God because he is, according to christian understanding, the eschatological presence of God. From the rational point of view, this is a possible and seriously justified interpretation of a historical event which is, because of its meaning (interpreted in the christian sense), authoritative for the believer who listens to the quiet voice of the historical event. The act by which this self-understanding is evoked, God's saving act in Christ, is therefore always understood at the same time in this new self-understanding. The existential and ontological pre-understanding of the revelation of being in the word helps us to see the existential interpretation of the bible at one and the same time as a christological and theological interpretation. Such an interpretation is neither a purely objective exposition which ignores the involvement of christian dogma in man's existence and results in pure orthodoxy in the unfavourable, rigid sense, nor a liberal interpretation which obscures the christological aspect.

We may therefore conclude that the signs of the universal manifestations of being in language, as expressed in different ways by philosophers, poets and other creative writers in history, dispose man to see in the event of Jesus the central and decisive manifestation of being. On the other hand the believer is also disposed, by his faith, to listen carefully to every form of language in which significant things are expressed.[25]

Finally, the christian interpretation of history, life in faith, implies living with the possibility, at least at the purely

rational level, that this faith may be an illusion. The interpretation is not rationally forceful and can only be verified
eschatologically.[26]

There are, however, sufficient reasons for regarding the
choice of faith as rationally and humanly justified. The believer may not have an absolute certainty, because the certainty of faith is not an evident and justified insight.

V Hermeneutic understanding and criteria of meaning in linguistic analysis

Whereas hermeneutics is basically a search for meaning, linguistic analysis, inspired by Leibnitz, looks for criteria of meaning and tries to establish them, at least insofar as there can be
any *a priori* limits set to the possible meaning of propositions.
The background and stimulus to this critical analysis of meaning is a criticism of ideology, which can therefore be compared
with the stimulus underlying the critical theory of society,
which will be discussed in the last two chapters of this book.

To begin with, linguistic analysts tried to find these criteria
in the logics of language. They went on to attempt to formulate empirical criteria and finally to look for pragmatic
criteria of meaning. The Oxford school especially claimed that
these pragmatic criteria could be found in ordinary language.
These logical, empirical and pragmatic criteria have also been
applied in various combinations, but the pragmatic criterion
of meaning has tended to predominate, especially in the definition that to understand a proposition is to understand its
language game, which means mastering the technique of the
language game: in other words, 'meaning is use'.

From the philosophical point of view, this raises certain
problems, for instance, if the language game—the church's
language of faith is a good example here—appears no longer
to function even among those who use it, the members of the
church themselves. (This problem is discussed more fully in
the next chapter.) Some philosophers believe that a new, pragmatic criterion of meaning is required in a case like this, although those of the Oxford school stick to the principle that
the criterion of meaning that can be applied to the use of
language is translatability into ordinary language.

The problem that concerns us here, however, is that of the
confrontation between the hermeneutics of being and the criticism of meaning in linguistic analysis.[27] It should be clear

from what has been said so far in this chapter that it is possible for pseudo-problems of hermeneutics to be exposed by linguistic analysis, both in the field of philosophy and in that of theology. According to the hermeneutics of being, the precondition of experience and of language is a non-explicit, pre-ontological understanding of being. According to the linguistic analysts, on the other hand, and especially according to Wittgenstein, language itself constitutes reality, with the result that it makes an understanding of being possible and indeed forms its basis. Since Wittgenstein, however, introduced the idea of the language game as a form of life, there is an inner affinity between the open pragmatism of forms of life and Heidegger's hermeneutics of being in the world. There is, on the other hand, a fundamental difference between them in that linguistic analysis reduces the reflectiveness of understanding to a technique.

It is nonetheless possible to speak of a bridge between linguistic analysis, with its idea of the language game, and hermeneutics, because the language of interpretation is in fact the language game of human history, the language of the past being made present in contemporary language in the hermeneutic process. The question then arises how it is possible to understand, in the light of an acquired language game, an alien language game and an alien form of life or society without the interpretation being a meta-language. I therefore agree with Apel[28] that this question is the same as the question of the conditions for a criticism of meaning in linguistic analysis. A hermeneutic language game—philosophy, for example—can be compared with a human conversation that is not yet closed or with the language game of human history.[29] This provides us with a much wider criterion of meaning, that of praxis, which in this case is the whole of man's history. In other words, another interpretation of reality is seen to underlie the criterion of meaning in linguistic analysis, a metaphysical presupposition.

According to linguistic analysis, every understanding of meaning presupposes that one forms a part of the language game. The context of this language game discloses a priori the structure of meaning. If one thinks in this light of a hermeneutic language game, that is, a language which is hermeneutically geared to another language game, it becomes clear that the interpreted language comes, precisely through the interpretation, to form a unity in dialogue with the interpreting language, so that both languages form a new language game. In this way, the meaning of one language game is interpreted in another language game and, in this case, not according to the norms of meaning and meaninglessness which are specific to the one language game, but in real diachronistic communication. This also brings us once again to the inevitable hermeneutic circle.

On the basis of the principle that language is a form of life, this wider criterion of meaning in praxis will enable us to examine the question of the practical and critical intention of hermeneutics as well as that of ortho-praxis as the basis of valid interpretation.

4
THEOLOGICAL CRITERIA

Not only in the Netherlands, but also throughout the whole world, and not only among ordinary christians, but also among the leaders of the churches, there is at present such pluralism in faith and in moral concepts that many different 'fronts' have been formed, cutting across the frontiers of the various churches. Quite often no open dialogue takes place between these different fronts. Sociological surveys have revealed that about 15 to 20% of christians are generally speaking conservative in their attitude, while another 15 to 20% are resolutely progressive. The great mass of people in between these two extremes, the group known to sociologists as the 'floating mass', generally follow, perhaps not with deep conviction, but certainly with consent, the course set by the church leaders. The attitude of the episcopate in any given country is therefore decisive with regard to the direction taken by the great 'floating mass'. If the bishops are conservative in their attitude, then the progressive minority will feel obliged to form 'underground churches'. If, on the other hand, the hierarchy has, without abandoning its supervision or *episkope*, a sympathetic or at least a neutral attitude towards the course followed by the progressives, the floating majority of christians will remain open to the progressive movement while the conservatives will tend to form underground churches where 'pure', 'orthodox' faith is preserved. It is not difficult to think of countries where the christian community fits into one or other of these two categories, but the most meaningful comments about this situation can be made by sociologists and socio-psychologists.

My only intention in this chapter is to reflect, as a believer, about the fact of pluralism in the world, a fact which the christian church simply cannot escape if it is really, although perhaps, critically, in the world. I shall therefore by-pass the psychological personality structure which so often plays a part both in the conservative and in the progressive attitude and which so often threatens to obscure the real problem because it leads to closed party positions and from these even to religious wars, possibly public, within the church. I shall also ignore the head in the sand policy of those who think that all that the theologians need to do at this time of universal unrest in the church is to remain silent for a while. After all, this means, in sober language, closing your eyes for a little while to the real questions that are being asked and pretending that nothing is the matter. It is in any case not the theologians who create the problems—they formulate the real questions which arise from the lives of believers themselves and are a real challenge to the traditional proclamation of faith. If this is overlooked, we inevitably practise double thinking; in other words, we are on the one hand forced—we hope without ideology—to admit that we are defeated by the insights of the empirical sciences, while on the other we as believers continue to cherish as a sacred pledge pre-critical and naive ideas of faith. This attitude is essentially untrue and un-christian and shows a lack of respect for the authentic word of God.

I propose, then, to consider theologically only this pluralism as a fact which can no longer be ignored and which compels us to reflect seriously about what is habitually known as orthodoxy or 'right faith'. I shall not ask the critical question of what place christianity occupies within the whole of humanity, both believing (in pluriformity) and non-believing, although this is a very serious question which is put to theologians by those who specialise in the study of missions and comparative religion as well as by those who are concerned with the problems of world communications. My point of departure will be *faith* in the christian interpretation of life and I shall confine myself to the factual problem of pluralism among those who confess Jesus the Christ as the norm for their living.

I Fundamental theological norms

A. CHRISTIAN FAITH CAUSES US TO THINK

1 In saying that 'faith comes from what is heard' (Rom 10:17) —*fides ex auditu*—Paul wanted to throw light on an essential aspect of faith, namely that it is not a thinking out of what could be thought out. Christian faith certainly causes us to *think*, but it is not thought out by us. It *causes* us to think. Believing is receiving what could not have been thought out by men. Thinking in faith is always thinking afterwards, reflecting about what has been heard. Philosophy is the fruit of reflection, of an analysis of an existential experience which causes us to think. Faith, on the other hand, is essentially what is not thought of itself, but rather promised to us, and this, which has not been thought out, claims our thought. What we have received in this way has, as it were, a lead or an advantage and we cannot catch it up by our thinking. If the object of theological reflection is therefore that which I do not have at my disposal, then it is clear that theology is tied to the previously given word of God. This is the *a priori* condition of all christian theology.[30]

2 This is, however, only one aspect of the truth. We do not, after all, hear a strange divine word in revelation. God's word is above all a human word, spoken by real men in their own language. In his book *The Secular Meaning of the Gospel*, Paul van Buren claimed that biblical talk about God in connection with Jesus Christ was really, logically and intentionally identical with the confirmation of Jesus' ultimate and unique significance *for us*.[31] From the point of view of linguistic analysis, this is perfectly acceptable and we can accept it without having at the same time to accept theologically the reduction to a human level implied in this view, which does not necessarily follow. Revelation reaches us through our interpretation of history in belief, although the direction taken by this interpretation is brought about by revelation itself. Revelation can only be recognised where man questions himself and interprets human language. God's word is given only in the human word and above all in the human word of Jesus. This is why revelation includes the human question of meaning. Speaking about God is at the same time a special way of speaking about man and his world. The theologians of secularisation are quite right about this. In the man Jesus, it is clear that revelation is accomplished in humanity. God's

revelation of himself takes place in the human situation of
Jesus. Jesus' human existence *is* meaningful speech about God's
communication of himself. Jesus interprets his own human
life and in so doing interprets God's revelation in an original
manner. The interpretative environment of revelation is therefore the full authenticity of humanity and interhumanity.
In this, those who practise the existential interpretation of the
bible are quite right.[32] The theological linguistic problem is
really not whether and to what extent the word of God can be
expressed in a human word, but rather whether and to what
extent human existence—itself the source of human language
—can express the mystery of God and his activity.

God's revelation therefore points in the first instance to the
mystery of man and ultimately to the man Jesus. It was
through Christ's entry into the *profundiora humanitatis* that
the *profundiora Dei* were revealed in him. Jesus' descent into
the depths of the hell of humanity, but also into the depths of
authentic humanity itself is, in this world, Jesus the *epiphaneia*
or manifestation of God. This is the structure itself of our
authentic listening to revelation and not simply a newfangled
demand made by capricious contemporary hermeneutics. Only
a real and authentic concern for our fellow-men and therefore
for the meaning of human existence can really give meaning
to the objective truths of the christian creed. As Hans Fortmann rightly said: 'When we speak, for example, about the
redemption, we shall have little chance of being heard by contemporary man and of receiving his consent as long as the
reality of that redemption is not visible, at least as a possibility, within his own life',[33] in other words, visible within the
historical dimension of our human and social life.

3 But this is also only a half truth, because the fact that God
can only reveal himself to us in a human manner, in the man
Jesus, means that, in Jesus, the human element itself not only
manifests God, but also at the same time conceals him. Historically, the figure of the man Jesus is ambiguous. Every
revelatory manifestation of God in and through the human
element, even in Jesus' humanity, is infinitely inadequate to
God himself, who is revealed in it. Although it is a revelation
of God, this human element, and indeed everything human,
always conceals God to some extent. This is why even Jesus'
humanity has the character not only of a manifestation, but
also, because of this concealment, of a reference which trans-

cends the purely human element. It is, in other words, also a
reference to God's infinite transcendence, which is not ab-
sorbed in the human manifestation. In the human measure of
Jesus—and this should be carefully considered—*God* becomes
accessible to us. This is why christianity resists every effort to
reduce the phenomenon of Jesus in our human history. The
Council of Chalcedon aimed at preventing a reduction of this
kind by speaking of the 'two natures' in Jesus Christ. The
Fathers of that council were not directly concerned with abstract metaphysics—this was, purely by chance, the referential
framework—but rather had an all-embracing existential
problem in mind: can and may a *man*, however exalted he
may be, claim our unconditional surrender without at the
same time forcing us into a depersonalising form of idolatry?
It is for this reason that, despite our acceptance of Jesus' full
humanity, his unique relationship with the Father is central
in the new testament. A christian faith without God has nothing to do with christianity.

All this can be expressed in many different ways. Even the
christian language of our fellow-believers may surprise us.

B. THE PROBLEM OF PLURALISM IN FAITH
1 Different languages for one revelation
It is precisely on the basis of this situation that the problem
of theological interpretation has arisen. All christians receive
the same revelation of God in Christ, but what they receive is
not expressed in the same way. What is received, what has
not been thought out by men, transcends all human possibility of expression. Thus each of the synoptic gospels presents
us with a somewhat different view of Christ or christology; as
a whole, the synoptic christology is very different from that
of Paul, and John's view of Christ seems, at first sight, almost
to take us into an entirely different world of faith. This pluralism is nonetheless accepted and sanctioned in and through the
church's understanding of faith in the 'canon' of the biblical
books. What is expressed in this is that it is only the totality
of these different biblical views of Christ, with their amplifica-
tion and criticism of each other, which can indicate the direction which orthodox interpretation of Christ must take. For
example, a representative of the Petrine and hellenistic tradition in the bible said (in 2 Pet 3: 15–16) that Paul's interpre-

tation was not easy to understand. Anyone who identifies the formulations of one particular understanding of faith with the revelation of God in Christ is, in the light of the canon of this biblical totality, guilty of the 'heresy of his own orthodoxy'. This special danger is most clearly revealed in ecumenical relationships. If one limited system of expression is identified with the revelation of God, orthodoxy has, in my opinion, become heresy.[34] Over and against this, I affirm that the demand of 'orthodoxy' consists in full trust in the biblical Jesus, the Christ in whom the act of salvation of God is accomplished in us. This 'orthodoxy' remains the hall-mark of all christian theology and no theologian who is worthy of the name would be prepared to give it up. It is not this trust, but its concrete expression or articulation which poses all kinds of new problems, especially in our own time. It is this that I should like to discuss in broad outline now.

2 Theological pluralism is pluralism in faith

There has, of course, always been the pluralism of theological schools in the church. Nowadays, however, we have to do with a different form of this pluralism. In the past, it operated within a common framework of assumptions and of questioning. The concepts, the philosophical presuppositions, and the Latin language were more or less common to everybody. The situation is different now, however. Philosophy itself has become pluralistic and the modern sciences have become independent sectors, each with its own sphere of meaning, and are no longer determined in any way by philosophy. The theologian has therefore to engage in direct dialogue with all these sciences. In the positive sciences, pre-reflective experience, in which the phenomenologists believed that they could find the final answer to the problems of philosophy, has been to some extent demythologised and exposed as a pre-scientific, naive experience with a pre-philosophical understanding of man and the world. This world of pre-reflective experience to a very great extent consists of the prejudices of people who have never come into contact with any science. (This is not to say that, within their own language games, such pre-scientific experiences are incorrect or meaningless as far as the understanding of everyday life is concerned.) In addition to this, the historical past, which the theologian must also investigate, has also become too great to measure. Such severe demands are made by the various methods, for example, the hermeneutic complications, the pruning knife of linguistic analysis and structuralist linguistics, that no theologian can in fact use all these methods, not even theologians working in a team. Finally, theology also requires the positive contribution of the humane and behavioural sciences.

The consequence of this is that a theologian, or even a group of theologians working together, has no more than a limited and one-sided view of the totality of the reality of faith, both qualitatively and quantitatively. Because of this, no theologian can say that what he does not see is theologically irrelevant, or even less important than what he has himself discovered. In this way, theological pluralism is bound to develop more and more, and theologians are bound to realise that, on the basis of the factors that I have mentioned, pluralism is simply inevitable and, in this sense, impossible to overcome. Or at least one is bound to say that successive attempts to form a bridge between the plurality of views results in new pluralism, *ad infinitum*. Other theologians know what we do not know and vice versa. Different theologies thus come about inevitably.

Furthermore, as we know, others have different and to us surprising points of departure. We can, of course, assimilate these surprising basic assumptions and to some extent incorporate them into our own thinking, but we are also aware of the limits of this possibility. Reading articles by our fellow theologians, for example, listening to what young people say, and hearing the views of intellectuals who are not professional theologians about faith, we are often bound to say: 'How strange! I think differently, but I cannot say with absolute certainty that this "strange" aspect is a departure from christian orthodoxy as I see it (and how can I see it in any other way?) because, although I cannot regard it as my own view (probably because of my own basic assumptions) I am conscious of something which prevents me from simply saying no to it.' It is frequently difficult either to accept or to reject the views of fellow theologians. We feel that such a view contains something strange, something that is not our own, but sometimes we are implicitly aware of what is potentially our own in what the other is saying. Even if this other person is making a frontal attack against an official doctrine of the church or denying it completely, it is often difficult to ascertain precisely what he is attacking. Is it what the doctrine contains according to his own (mistaken) interpretation, or precisely what the doctrine intends to say and does in fact say, possibly within certain definite presuppositions which are strange to us? And have we ourselves fully understood that doctrine, situated it sufficiently within its own historical sphere of understanding and then compared it with the other spheres of understanding in scripture and the church's tradition of faith, so that we are really able to distil its precise meaning from all this? If the affirmative and the negative replies are distinctly opposed to each other, and this within the same reflected sphere of understanding, then our judgement about orthodoxy or heterodoxy is easy and even inevitable. At the moment, however, the difficulty is that there are, in addition to the theology that each person accepts as his own, and which is always tending to shift its position, other theologies which claim to express the same christian profession of faith theologically with a seriousness, a conscientiousness and a professional skill that are in no way inferior to our own.

Goodwill alone is not, of course, enough. On the other hand it should not be forgotten that the christian profession of faith is only presented in a theological interpretation. Faith and the theological understanding of faith cannot be so clearly separated as many think. Theological pluralism always implies pluralism in the understanding of the christian profession of faith itself. If, then, theological pluralism exists, as it evidently does nowadays, the question arises of how we can make sure that the other person is professing the same christian faith when his theology, because of other implicit presuppositions, is strange by comparison with our own, and if this theology which strikes us as strange claims to be as authentic an understanding of the faith as our own. Anyone who is well versed in the bible will not be fundamentally disturbed by this question, because he will already be acquainted with the pluralism of the christian understanding of faith that is present in scripture. All the same, the modern phenomenon of pluralism may still trouble even the christian who is versed in the bible, because the bible certainly does not contain all the possible forms of christian pluralism. This contemporary pluralism far transcends the pluralism that is encountered in the bible.

A clear example of unresolved pluralism is the difference

between the Dutch *New Catechism* and the 'Roman' view of what has been expressed in Jesus Christ. In this, I am not alluding to the more superficial errors made on both sides, but to the very heart of the matter. Despite their obvious goodwill, it is clear that the 'Roman' theologians are unable to grasp and assess the philosophical presuppositions and the differently orientated and more existentially based thought which underlies the Dutch Catechism. As a consequence, any dialogue between the Dutch and the 'Roman' theologians time and again ends in deadlock. On the other hand, the Dutch theologians are generally speaking able to grasp and assess the 'Roman' presuppositions because they themselves have been through 'Roman' scholasticism. In principle, of course, mutual understanding is undoubtedly possible, but what can be done if this understanding turns out to be impossible in practice? In view of the human situation, it is hardly surprising that it does often prove to be impossible nowadays. Even if a third group of theologians were able to trace, by reflection, both these opposing positions—the Dutch and the 'Roman'—back to their presuppositions, and in this way establish, again by reflection, that they are both identical as far as faith is concerned, the question would still arise whether this third authority could in fact come to such a judgement in all cases. If it could not establish any identity of faith and felt obliged to accuse another theological position—for example, that of a Paul van Buren—of deviating from christianity, is it then not possible that it might unconsciously have come into contact with the impossibility which we encountered just now, the impossibility of grasping and assessing the other position because of its own implicit or explicit presuppositions? No one can fully think out and trace back his own presuppositions, let alone those of another person. For this reason, everything seems to point to the fact that a purely theoretical verification of orthodoxy or heterodoxy is simply impossible. It does, however, happen that interpretations of faith which were condemned by the teaching office of the church in the past have been rehabilitated after a time, because it has generally come to be understood that the writer concerned had put forward his ideas on the basis of implicit philosophical (and sometimes almost purely linguistic) presuppositions which were different from those which had played a part in the theological understanding of the church's teaching office. In fact,

because positions tend to harden as a result of their opposition
to each other and because of the 'swing of the pendulum' in
history, the 'orthodoxy' of one century is very often the pre-
lude to the 'heresy' of the following period and vice versa.

It is therefore impossible to provide an answer to the problem of orthodox re-interpretation which will be completely
satisfactory from the theological point of view. If this were
possible, it would certainly disprove the fact of a pluralism
that is impossible to overcome. We must not, of course, simply
record this pluralism just as a fact. There is always an urgent
need for us to examine our own sphere of understanding
critically and to enlarge it and to learn from others in dialogue. We have, however, also become aware of the limits of
dialogue and have learnt to realise that becoming conscious
of modern pluralism in theology is equal to becoming conscious of the inevitable human situation of theology in the
church. Pluralism is an aspect of the historical reality of man
and cannot ultimately be overcome. At least one is bound
to say that this pluralism must be overcome again and again
in the future, but that this act of overcoming pluralism is a
process which will never cease here on earth.

3 The limits of pluralism and of its removal
Pluralism is not absolute. Even though there is no identity
between the various views, there is certainly the possibility of
communication and therefore of a certain verification. As the
later Wittgenstein maintained, a private language is in principle impossible.[35] That unknown languages and language
games can in principle be translated and therefore can be
understood is a fact. When archaeologists made a strange discovery and later identified this as cuneiform writing, the
written form of a language, it also became possible to understand and translate this language. There are logical structures
which are universally valid and which therefore make communication between different interpretations of reality possible. Anyone constructing his own language for the purpose
of expressing experiences which are only accessible to him—
for example, the pain which only he experiences—would not
be able to provide a criterion of true linguistic usage. He
would therefore not be able to be understood. Unless language
is related to a public verifying authority, it cannot be understood, translated, proved true or subjected to hermeneutics.

The discovery of truth has an essentially social character and the affirmation of truth is therefore impossible without a social institution. Language, in other words, the language game with its own rules, also clearly has the structure of a social institution, to which we are subject in giving and interpreting meaning.

It is being able to participate in a common language game with public rules that can be verified by everyone that makes all understanding and hermeneutics possible. The fact that man clearly has this possibility at his disposal means that pluralism cannot be the last word. Mankind is essentially a community of communication or, as Royce and Peirce have expressed it, a 'community of interpretation'.[36] Being conscious of pluralism in fact means implicitly transcending it because, in that case, one does not regard one's own frame of thought as exclusive. But even if the fact that every language or every other person's interpretation can in principle be translated and therefore understood is in itself a step towards overcoming pluralism, translation remains, as everyone knows, difficult and very few translations may really be called completely successful. Compared with the original text, all translations are either under-exposed or over-exposed. It is also often true, where a translation is not quite successful, that there was something wrong with the meaning of the original text, although the author usually blames the translator for failing to understand his meaning. There are limits to any attempt to overcome pluralism. The contemporary dialogue, which all of us hold in high esteem, has nonetheless made all of us more conscious than ever before of these limits.

II The criteria for continuity in the orthodox understanding of faith

Certain catholics are no doubt of the opinion that the only direct and safe guarantee, in the case of a pluralism which is apparently impossible to overcome, is the pastoral teaching office of the church. The question, however, is whether this office can by a mere word of authority by-pass the dialectics which exist in the community of faith and which are directed towards the question of truth. I have already mentioned that the christian profession of faith cannot be expressed separately from a (special) theological language. Even the official pronouncements of the church imply a theology and, what is more, one of many theologies. From the purely theoretical point of view it cannot be directly and adequately determined to what extent the many theologies really come together in a single christian profession of faith. The difficulty, then, is that if the teaching office of the church takes up a position, this position is to some extent borne up by one theology which exists alongside other theologies which also claim to express the same faith. How, then, can the question of truth be decided magisterially? Some theologians maintain that this can be done by the official charisma of the teaching authority of the church. I do not wish to deny that the Holy Spirit can and does help the church and her leaders charismatically, but I do not think that the actual decisions, which are the pronouncements of the church, can be explained directly by this charismatic help of the Spirit. To do this would be to get out of the real difficulties for which an ecclesiological explanation ought to be supplied by making a kind of miraculous appeal to the help of the Holy Spirit. It is only when the internal course of a decision made by the teaching office of the church has been analysed and, insofar as free human decisions can ever be fully fathomed, to some extent clarified that one can really discern the activity of the Spirit in this decision or the human failure to respond to God's grace. Anyone who analyses the internal structure of such magisterial decisions objectively is at the same time paying homage to the Holy Spirit, who is sometimes active despite human failure. Before examining the real meaning of the role of the church's teaching office, therefore, we must first clarify all kinds of other internal factors.

The problem which ultimately presents itself is this. In view of the theological pluralism which confronts us as believers, what is the criterion which is able to guarantee 'orthodoxy' or the correct understanding of faith? What is the principle of verification, on the basis of which a correct reinterpretation of faith can be distinguished from an 'heretical' interpretation? In other words, what is the criterion on the basis of which we can recognise, in this pluralism of faith, different theological interpretations of the same christian profession of faith, insofar as this is distinguished from nonchristian interpretations?

Thinkers of the schools of linguistic analysis have undoubtedly done a great deal towards finding a solution to this problem. Unlike those who belong to the purely theoretical, hermeneutic tradition of the humanities—I am referring here to those who take the 'hermeneutic circle' as their point of departure, from Schleiermacher and Dilthey via Heidegger to Bultmann, the post-Bultmannian school and Gadamer—they look for a principle by which they are able to verify the correctness or incorrectness of theological reinterpretation. Again and again they ask the provoking question: 'How do you know?', and do not remain satisfied with the rather mysterious distinction that the others make between 'what is said' and 'what is meant'. According to this Bultmannian distinction, the strange quality is attributed to an author of never in fact saying what he really means and never meaning what he in fact says. The comfortable consequence of this for the interpreter is that he can insert his own meanings into the text, and it seems fully justified because the text did not in fact say what it intended to say, whatever that might have been. With the help of this distinction, theologians rather questionably seem to deduce the very opposite of what a father of the church or a pronouncement of the Council of Trent, for example, really said. A fifth-century church father can, in this way, be given the appearance of a twentieth-century existentialist thinker. Paul van Buren has rightly asked why we demythologise the God of the bible and not the gods of Olympus. This sally is only intended to emphasise that, unless he is writing a satire or to puzzle or in some other special literary genre, an author generally says what he means and means what he says. Within a certain language game, the meaning of what is said is open to the one to whom the words are addressed. Of course, no author succeeds completely in this aim, because he has to say what he means in 'alienation', that is, in language, and this also includes objective structures in which his ideas have to be objectivised and, so to speak, dispossessed. What is more, all kinds of presupposition play a part in the author's thought. These certainly do not form the central core of his meaning, but they are nonetheless, in his particular situation, indissolubly connected with it to such an extent that, apart from them, he would simply not be able to signify his real meaning. (We have only to think here, for example, of the opponents of Galileo.)

Unlike the one-sided concentration of the purely theoretical hermeneutics of Western Europe, whose supporters regard not the meaning of the text, but our contemporary under-standing of it, as a problem, the Anglo-Saxon analytical philo-sophers of America, Britain and Scandinavia see the problem not in terms of our understanding of the text, but of the meaning itself. May one, *a priori*, take the proposition that the text to be interpreted is meaningful and therefore auth-oritative for one's point of departure?[37] As the linguistic analysts correctly maintain, all insights of public importance are subject to public control. This applies equally well to philosophical and theological speculation about ultimate ques-tions (even though it is quite different to say that the criteria of the positive sciences are normative for the meaningful character of philosophical and theological statements, which is apparently the point of departure for many linguistic analysts). The question of meaning and of our interpretative understand-ing of that meaning can only be answered if we at the same time, and in a particular case, answer the question of the criteria for meaning and consequently for the understanding of that meaning. This aspect of the problem has often been over-looked by the members of the Western European hermeneutic school.

Schoonenberg has rightly said: 'If there is to be a com-munity of faith, this must be able to recognise itself in plural-ism, so that the different movements are able to hear the same message at least approximately in each others' language and thought'.[38] This is not only true, it is also fundamental to our problem. It will, however, be necessary to establish certain criteria, on the basis of which an approximate recognition of this kind will be genuinely possible and not remain simply a pious wish. To be able socially to recognise the truth is not constitutive for truth, but it is essential to man's discovery of truth. I shall now try to formulate several criteria, without attempting to be exhaustive.

A. THE CRITERION OF THE PROPORTIONAL NORM

From the purely theological point of view, orthodoxy cannot be verified. A purely theoretical form of hermeneutics, even one of the existentially theoretical kind, based on a study of the humanities, such as that of Gadamer, cannot solve this problem adequately. A purely theoretical verification can only be an eschatological event,[39] but the theologian who wants to write a book about the christian interpretation of reality here

on earth cannot wait for this. All the same, faith in this
eschatological verification is still important because it situates
our theological interpretative understanding of faith within
the hope which transcends all rational evidence or doubt,
assurance or alarm. This has the effect of exposing the deadly
seriousness with which the modern theologians of renewal
practise, almost exclusively, hermeneutics or linguistic analysis
and study structuralism, and of making it to some extent relative for genuine believers. The authentic interpretation of
faith is not a theoretical conclusion, but an act of God-centred
hope which will always be associated with rational doubts. It
should also not be forgotten that, as far as this question is
concerned, believers and non-believers are both in the same
boat. The believer's interpretation of reality does not have to
be any more emphatically 'justified' than that of the non-
believer. The interpretations of both are, after all, open to the
criticism of both. But they do have, probably in different
gradations, sufficient grounds for justifying their basic choice
to some extent from the human, rational (and therefore also
moral) point of view.

But, quite apart from the pluralism which cannot be overcome, a purely theoretical verification of a particular interpretation of faith is also impossible because although the
object of faith has indeed been realised, in Christ, it has only
been realised as our promise and our future, and the future
cannot be interpreted theoretically, it has to be brought about.
Action (orthopraxis) must therefore be an inner element of
the principle of verification. Christianity is not a purely hermeneutic undertaking or a question of pure *theoria*; it is ultimately a question of action in faith.

On the other hand, however, even the pragmatists tend to
by-pass the goal here, because human action is, in every sphere,
inconceivable without some theoretical implication. Similarly,
christian orthopraxis is also inconceivable without an element
of theoretical christian knowledge and, in that sense, of orthodoxy.

There is, especially in contemporary protestant religious
philosophy, a tendency to speak about the 'a-theoretical' character of the christian profession of faith and to separate completely the question of meaning from the question of truth.
But even if no purely theoretical verification can be made, the
process of verifying orthodox christian life as a whole does

contain a theoretical element. A purely wordless profession of
faith simply does not exist. Religious speech, with its strange
logic, consists of speaking about the inexpressible, because
what is peculiar about the inexpressible, by comparison with
mere 'nothing', is that it is in fact spoken about. Revelation
attains its fulfilment precisely as revelation when it is expressed and spoken about, just as in the whole of human life
it is only through language that things become publicly revealed and enter the sphere of 'revelation', towards which man
has to direct his responsibility as a speaking subject. Revelation is God's saving action in history insofar as it is expressed
and spoken about. The history of salvation had been expressed
in language in the bible and in the christian profession of
faith.

In asking about 'orthodox' faith, it is therefore impossible to
ignore the question of the meaning of the concepts of and the
statements about faith. This must not, however, be answered
in the way in which theologians in the past traced the problem
of orthodoxy or heterodoxy back to an affirmation about the
'unchangeable' element in faith and a 'new' element. This
solution was based on a misunderstanding of the structure of
the act of faith, which contains a correlation between the
saving mystery of Christ and the basic intentionality or orientation of the act of faith which is inwardly determined by the
mystery of Christ. Christian faith is not a neutral, previously
given structure, which can afterwards be directed towards
the saving mystery of Christ. If faith is basically correctly
orientated, it is inwardly determined by the mystery of Christ.
The concepts and formulations of faith are therefore, as expressions, correlative not only to the mystery of Christ, but
also to the deeper intentionality of the act of faith. What one
believes (*fides quae*) can never be adequately distinguished from
the fact that one believes (*fides qua*). This orthodox faith, or
the correct orientation of faith, must also be recognised to
some extent in the concept of faith and it must above all be
recognised on the basis of the first and normative expression
of the believing community, scripture. Yet it is precisely this
expression of 'orthodox' faith in the concepts of faith which
cannot be theoretically verified. A contemporary form of
orthodoxy should imply that it is precisely in the plural interpretation of faith that the meaning of God's word of revelation can be heard. The study of the development of dogma

and of the history of theology has provided us with a number of rules, criteria or norms which can help us in this. They present us with a series of understandable or intelligible structures, the result of various attempts to set the whole of christian existence, its experiences, convictions and professions of faith, intellectually in order, with the help of the achievements that are available in society at a certain time. These structures arise from the confluence of basic elements of faith (the biblical *kerygma*) and structurising elements taken from a given social and cultural context.[40] On the one hand, then, there are changes, never completely discontinuous, which imply a remarkable growth in these structurising elements and, on the other hand, the elements of faith are approached from the vantage-point of various spiritual experiences. The combination of the structurising framework and the data of faith thus structurised results in what can be called 'structures', that is, expressions of the christian experience in a given period, understandably ordered in an intelligible framework. This experience is itself inspired by the proclamation of the bible, because, as I have already said, even the kerygmatic datum itself can never be contained in a wordless gesture which precedes all conceptual expression.

If the various structures that have arisen in the course of history are compared with each other and, in this comparison, the key words of the biblical proclamation are taken as a referential framework, we certainly become aware of 'structural rules' which—even if the structure has lost its efficacy in a different social context—still preserve their intelligibility as models for every new structurisation. In this way, we can deduce constant but purely proportional principles which will be a safe guide for our interpretation of faith. Given the referential framework of the philosophy of the fourth and fifth centuries for example, the definition of Chalcedon that Christ has two natures but one person is bound to be the assured answer to the question of Christ's identity. What is more, anyone attempting to answer the same question now within the same philosophical framework would also be bound to answer it in precisely the same way, if he did not want to misrepresent the idea of Christ. In this way, the authority of God's word continues to have an effect in the church's formulation, while this formulation as such is always dependent on time and place and is therefore also relative. The norm is therefore proportional, consisting in the relationship between the intentionality of faith and a given (and changing) referential framework. The relationship must also remain the same in different referential frameworks. This means, therefore, that the truth that was expressed in the definition of Chalcedon must remain sound in every other referential framework which structurises the datum of faith. The criterion for orthodox faith is therefore not an unchangeable formula and not even a homogeneous one, just as, on the other hand, any new character is no indication as such of a wrong development in faith. The criterion consists of a certain proportion in which subsequent expressions (in their different contexts) find themselves with regard to the intentionality of faith as inwardly determined by the mystery of Christ. In conceptual expression, it should be possible to recognise a reflection of the balance that exists in the mystery of Christ and the christian experience of faith. The constant relationship that there is between the changing understandable structures and any aiming at or referring to the mystery indicates the direction that every re-interpretation should take. At the level of theory, all that we have at our disposal, then, is a proportional norm— models of structurisation of faith, of which scripture supplies the first and therefore the normative ones.[41] Because of its proportional character, the criterion for orthodox faith can therefore never be thought out purely theoretically. This criterion always refers to something other than itself; in it is revealed the transcendence of the mystery over pure theory. The theoretical criterion of verification therefore inwardly requires, because it is insufficient, other criteria which should also be able to ensure theological verification of an interpretation of faith. Our concepts do not embrace the reality in themselves; their orthodoxy can only be judged if they are seen as bound up with the whole life of faith inspired by a correct orientation towards the saving mystery of Christ. They have to participate in this intentionality, but this can take place in many different (proportionally equal) ways. On the basis of the plural expressions as such, no definitive or conclusive decisions can be made either for or against their christian orthodoxy.

However inadequate they may be, the concepts and the professions of faith therefore have the character of a cognitive reference and this is an inward element of what I call the whole of the principle of verification. The word comes to us and is nonetheless expressed and discussed by us as if we were its masters, with consequent restrictions in our expressions of it. Precisely because this element of appropriation in the total process of coming or bringing to expression involves 'restrictions', the result could be plurality: from the one gospel, there arises a gospel according to Mark, Matthew, Luke and John and an interpretation of this according to Augustine and Athanasius and then according to Thomas and so on, in an unending series. What manifests itself to us in gratuitous revelation goes beyond the filter of our human language: speaking about faith is the subjection of man to that which shows and gives itself and at the same time the 'guarding' in human speech (to use Heidegger's word) of what wants to make itself understood.

The theoretical element in the interpretation of faith is therefore important; faith cannot be arbitrarily interpreted in any way one likes. On the other hand, the purely theoretical aspect of the illumination of faith in itself is not sufficient as a verification of the orthodoxy of faith. This aspect of knowledge only functions within the totality of christian existence and praxis. The community in the one faith does not come about separately from the word of faith, but the word of faith does not, on the other hand, form the totality of this community in faith.[42] The realities of faith are never present separate from the word, but they are not identical with it. The word of faith is not the total and exclusive foundation of the one community in faith. Communal liturgy and communal christian care for the building up of a better world are not sufficient, separate from the word of faith, to verify the orthodoxy of faith. On the other hand, because of the presuppositions which also play a part it is just as impossible to determine the orthodoxy of faith purely on the basis of a theoretical assertion that concepts of faith formulated in a pluralist manner nevertheless contain the same intentionality.

B. THE CRITERION OF CHRISTIAN ORTHOPRAXIS

In the hermeneutics of, for example, the Bultmannian and post-Bultmannian school, an irreplaceable function is fulfilled by the idea of 'pre-understanding' in the interpretation of texts from the past. The simple fact that Bultmann appeals to the earlier Heidegger of *Sein und Zeit,* but Ebeling and

Fuchs appeal to the later Heidegger for the content of this pre-understanding shows the extent to which the christian message is subjected to a particular philosophy. The difficulty which I see as presenting us with a powerful argument against such a conception of pre-understanding as a hermeneutical principle in our own times is the very fact of philosophical pluralism. The christian faith is faced with a multiplicity of positive views of man. On what can christian theologians, such as Bultmann and his followers, base their choice of Heidegger's philosophy as the best and therefore the most suitable for a christian interpretation of the bible?[43] In doing this, surely very many people, who have a different positive view of man, are excluded from an understanding of the biblical message?

Is this subjection of the christian message to one particular philosophy in a pluralistic society not an essential limitation of the universal intelligibility of the gospel, which is, after all, directed towards the salvation of the whole of mankind? There is, in addition to Heidegger's pre-understanding, a French understanding—*la philosophie de la reflexion*—a Sartrian view of man, an Anglo-Saxon pre-understanding, an interpretation of man according to Unamuno, and all this quite apart from the non-Western views of man. Everything points to the fact that the concept 'pre-understanding', at least in the way in which it is used by theologians with an appeal to existential hermeneutics, leads us into a blind alley, certainly as far as a scientific theology is concerned which makes some claim to be universal. (A different judgement would, of course, be possible in the case of preaching geared to a specific situation.) What is more, every positive idea of man is in fact not only a mixture of experiences and of a correct thematisation of these experiences, but also a collection of various hypotheses together with speculation and even pure ideology. How can one of the many positive views of man, then, form the basis for the pre-understanding of christianity? This would in fact mean the introduction in advance of the principle of reduction into the theological interpretation of faith and the result would be a reduction of christianity itself. A positive view of man cannot, at least theologically, provide the pre-understanding for a true interpretation of faith. All the same, there must somewhere be a pre-understanding, otherwise the gospel will present itself as unintelligible gibberish.

If we look for what is common to the many positive views of man, then we are struck at once by one element which is indeed common to them all, the expression of a non-thematis- able, positive sphere of meaning which cannot be concept- ualised but which is presupposed to all positive views of man: a negative dialectic, borne up and guided by a sphere of mean- ing.[44] As E. Bloch has said, in all positive views of man, man can be seen as seeking the threatened *humanum*. What this *humanum* is positively is only expressed in plural, fragmen- tary and mutually contradictory positive views of man, but this commitment to the threatened *humanum* is what can be found in all these plural forms and it is this that constitutes the universal pre-understanding of all these different views of man. A sphere of meaning is revealed in the negative experiences of contrast in our personal and social life, since such experience of contrast would be impossible without this. What is positive in it, however—the sphere of meaning—is only expressed in critical opposition to what is inhuman in the situation, while the positive expression of it disintegrates at once into pluralism. This critical attitude does not disavow the humanity that has already been attained; it is simply opposed to what has been attained if it shows a tendency to perpetuate itself and therefore threatens to inhibit what P. Ricoeur has called 'what is humanly desirable'. This negative dialectic within a one-sided sphere of meaning which cannot be conceptualised univocally forms, in my opinion, the uni- versal pre-understanding of the gospel, in which the believer does not have to subject himself to one particular philosophy. After all, universal salvation, which is proclaimed to all man- kind, with a special preference for the poor and underprivi- leged, and which is expressed in the gospel in the powerful symbol of the 'kingdom of God' (although this is done in a negative manner as a kingdom without evil or tears; see 2 Pet 3:13; Rev 21:4) is very closely connected with this human pre-understanding. The *humanum* which is sought, but always threatened, is proclaimed and promised in Jesus Christ. The kingdom of God is the *humanum* which is sought, but now promised in Christ, made conceivable and really assured for us in grace. On this universal basis of human pre- understanding, we can once again include the 'hermeneutic circle' and the correlation of question and answer (as asked by K. Barth, R. Bultmann, P. Tillich, G. Ebeling, G. Moltmann, W. Pannenberg and so on) in the theological interpretation, but in a different orientation.

Yet compared with the purely theoretical hermeneutics of the humanities, an essentially new element is introduced here into theological hermeneutics: orthopraxis or 'right doing'. It is not possible to affirm that we can interpret the past, in advance and purely theoretically, in the light of the present, in order then to interpret, for example, the one baptism, the one celebration of the eucharist and christian commitment to man and the world as pure consequence of a unity of faith which is already firmly established in advance and purely theoretically verified. Those who practise purely theoretical hermeneutics (Gadamer, Bultmann, Ebeling and Fuchs) affirm, correctly, that the past must be interpreted in the light of the present. The object of christian faith is, of course, already realised in Christ, but it is only realised in him as our promise and our future. But future cannot be theoretically interpreted, it must be done. The *humanum* which is sought and which is proclaimed and promised to us in Christ is not an object of purely contemplative expectation, but also a historical form which is already growing in this world: at least this is what we have to do, in the perspective of eschatological hope. Christianity is not simply a hermeneutic undertaking, not simply an illumination of existence, but also a renewal of existence, in which 'existence' concerns man as an individual person and in his social being.

In interpreting the past in the light of the present, then, it should not be forgotten that eschatological faith imposes on the present the task of transcending itself, not only theoretically, but also as a change to be realised. Only the critical attitude towards the present, and the resulting imperative to change and improve it, really open access to the coming truth. The basic hermeneutic problem of theology, then, is not so much the question of the relationship between the past (scripture and tradition) and the present, but between theory and practice, and this relationship can no longer be solved idealistically, by a theory of Kantian pure reason from which consequences flow for the practical reason, but it will have to be shown how the theory appears in the praxis itself. How, for example, can religious freedom, as formulated by Vatican II, be deduced by purely theoretical exegesis from the church's past? The church's practice in the past at least contradicts this theory rather seriously. Only a new praxis in the church can make the new interpretation credible, namely as a theoretical element in effective practice here and now by the churches themselves. Without the renewal of praxis in the church, there can be no historical basis for the re-interpretation. Indirectly, via the new praxis, this can still be formulated in a theory.

This fact alone shows that hermeneutics such as Gadamer's, based simply on a study of the humane sciences, will not suffice for theology. Christianity does not merely throw light on man's existence, it aims above all to renew that existence, and the *theoria* of christianity is an implicit element of this. The *doxa*, which may or may not be *orthos*, will therefore be found in christian orthopraxis. A misunderstanding of this fact can, for example, be found in 'existential interpretation of the bible', which postulated a schism between man's understanding of the world and his understanding of himself, claiming that the new testament understanding of the world is antiquated, but that its self-understanding is still valid. This, of course, resulted in the great programme of demythologisation, which was basically a separation of the self-understanding of the new testament from its antiquated understanding of the world. What was forgotten in this programme, however, was the fact that man can only really come to himself in the world, and that the image of the world and the image of man are so essentially connected with each other that, in changing the world, man also changes himself and thus acquires a new self-understanding. If, in other words, biblical understanding is in any way antiquated, then biblical self-understanding is also similarly antiquated. This implies that biblical self-understanding can only be elucidated with the help of biblical mythology, not by an elimination of that mythology. What is more, it is also clear that man's changing of the world today has an inner function to fulfil in throwing light on twentieth century christian self-understanding. An existential interpretation which ignores this will reduce christianity to an invisible salvation taking place in the private sphere of individual decision—this certainly was the case with Bultmann and even more so with Gogarten. The theology of secularisation is therefore basically a new ideology, leaving the world as it is and reducing salvation to the level of an intimate inner experience without influence on the world of human society and history. The consequence is that there is nothing left to interpret, because, apart from God's address to man, everything lies outside the scope of faith and the hermeneutic question is silent, confronted by the barrier of blind obedience in faith which withdraws from critical thinking into a safe area of pure theology.

Christian orthopraxis or 'right doing', then, is not a consequence of a previously given, communal unity of faith, but the manner in which such a communal unity and conviction is realised. The way in which this is effectively realised is also the conscious assurance of orthodoxy. The unity thus realised includes more than a unity within the conceptual or figurative pluralism of the word of faith. It is only if this orthopractical unity exists that the unity of the same faith and of the same profession of faith can also be known and recognised within the understanding of faith even if it is theologically divergent and pluralistically expressed. The christian creed was originally not a purely doctrinal or theoretical formulation of orthodoxy, but rather an integral part of the church's liturgy of baptism, in other words, the theoretical element of (and in) an action of the church. Similarly, in the case of other religions as well, saying (the myth and the saga) was implied in doing (the rite). Rite and myth mutually interpreted each other. If the creed is separated from its total context in the church or if it is identified with a theoretical doctrine which can be subjected to *hermeneia*, with all the latest novelties of purely theoretical hermeneutics, then the christian profession of faith is made unsuitable as a criterion for judging orthodoxy, partly because theological pluralism, precisely as an understanding of faith, is impossible to overcome. The great heresy which threatens all forms of christianity and which has laid fatal traps for it since the beginning is gnosticism, which narrows christianity down to a theoretical doctrine, consistent with its point of departure in leaving the world as it is, or to a hermeneutic clarification of existence without any concern for the effective renewal of the world or of man's existence. This heresy, which has frequently, of course, presented itself as 'orthodoxy', has haunted authentic christianity from its origins and throughout the centuries up to the present day, has laid snares for it and made it incredible for many people. Christians have again and again been ensnared by it and become heretics and have in turn made heretics of their fellow-believers. What is more, this is still taking place.

In a certain sense, it is never possible to say whether a purely theoretical theology is, in the true sense of the word, orthodox, really *orthos* or 'right' as far as faith is concerned. We know from linguistic analysis that the language game partly determines the meaning of the words that we use. This context also includes extra-linguistic elements, in other words, human behaviour. When a theologian such as Paul van Buren, for example, says that speaking about God is meaningless, but at the same time professes that Christ is our unique rule of life, then the really orthodox meaning of his statement, which is purely christological and explicitly not theological, is partly dependent on the influence that it has on his actual life. Van Buren's life will or will not show whether he accepts, according to truth, anything unique and absolute in Christ, despite the faulty conceptualisation of his conviction.[45] An orthopraxis of this kind can, moreover, be more orthodox in the christological sense, that is if one considers orthodoxy to be the theoretical implications of christian praxis, than the statement 'Jesus Christ is one person in two natures', if this profession of faith does not function in human behaviour. The meaning of a 'secular' statement such as 'Christ is our unique rule of life' is ultimately religious and fully christian, because the meaning of what is said within a given language game is also determined by the whole of human behaviour and cannot be determined purely theoretically. If the meaning of the profession of faith could be determined purely theoretically, then this would pose the unanswerable question: why accept this 'demythologisation' and not that one? From the purely theoretical point of view, I cannot see any satisfactory answer to this question, unless all kinds of unverifiable religious and pseudo-religious preferences act as arguments. In the sense of linguistic analysis, 're-interpretation' means speaking differently about the same thing, while preserving the intentionality of the bible. In this sense, too, heresy or incorrect interpretation does not mean speaking differently from the bible, but speaking about something other than the bible speaks about and interpreting this as speaking in faithfulness to the bible. In this sense, one is bound to admit that christians have spoken in word and deed incorrectly about the same thing. If one does not admit this, then all purely theoretical hermeneutics simply become a *tour de force* which no one can believe in.

All this has far-reaching consequences if the principles that I have outlined here, those of the pluralist understanding of faith within the one christian community of the church, are consistently applied to the phenomenon of pluralism in the various christian churches. This would be ecumenically fully justified, but it would take us too far. It would also require a far more detailed linguistic analysis of each other's theology.

C. THE CRITERION OF ACCEPTANCE BY THE PEOPLE OF GOD

Christian faith is the faith of a community which has a history in time and space and which interprets this in the light of the need to act consistently in a christian manner and in the light of changing (philosophical and social) assumptions. Christian proclamation takes place in a specific situation of discourse, which of course has a context of communication. The world of faith is a communal world, with a sphere of shared interest and also a world of shared speech and understanding—a 'universe of discourse'[46] Communication does not take place if the shared presuppositions are absent or are not consciously and reflectively discussed. This is why communication is only possible in the very act of interpretation. However many difficulties there may be in connection with this communication, the acceptance of a definite theological interpretation of faith by the community of faith, the church, forms an essential element in the whole of the criterion of verification. The subject sustaining the hermeneutics is not the individual theologian, but the community of the church as a whole.[47] This partial criterion of acceptance is, of course, not very practical at the moment when a theologian proposes a new interpretation. History teaches us that centuries may pass before the community of the church comes to recognise itself in a given interpretation of faith. To begin with, a new interpretation is more likely to be disputed and even declared heretical by the community than to be accepted, because of its surprising newness. So long as the church permits and encourages scientific freedom and openness and does not make a theologian suffer harm because of juridical regulations—in which case all theological discussion comes to an end—scientific criticism and counter-criticism arises. A new interpretation of this kind is often accepted by a considerable number in the community of the church, while another section of the community rejects it. In my opinion, the official church should respect this tested dialectical process within the community of faith. It is only after a great deal of friction that a new interpretation can be either accepted or rejected. In the course of this debate, naturally, all kinds of new problems will have arisen.

Acceptance of a new interpretation of faith does not necessarily mean a positive acceptance by the universal church. For example, the universal church does in fact accept the ideas about faith put forward by the Eastern catholic churches, which are constructed quite differently from those of the Western church and do not function as an interpretation of faith in the Latin church. Bizarre and eccentric opinions are, as it were, silently eliminated from the community of faith by the principle of acceptance of an interpretation, although a certain amount of noise may continue to be heard in more limited circles.

The significance of the acceptance of a new interpretation of faith by a local church should not be underestimated. The second Vatican Council affirmed that the universal church was made present here and now in the local church.[48] The other local churches, guided by their bishops, also live from the same gospel of Christ. These other churches' understanding of faith and evangelical inspiration also serves, for this reason, as a critical authority for the separate 'communities of God'. No local church can ever claim that its authentic experience is an exhaustive realisation of the whole of the gospel and of christian inspiration. The local communities of God are therefore essentially subject to the criticism of the other local churches and, ultimately, to that of all the leaders of the local churches with the 'president of the bond of love' among them—the bishop to whom the office of the primacy of Peter is entrusted within the college of bishops. Assuming this, then, the consciousness of faith of one local church which accepts a given interpretation of faith may well be a *locus theologicus,* a source for theology within the universal church, an indication of the Holy Spirit, on the basis of which the given interpretation may indeed be regarded as a safe guiding principle.

Acceptance by the community of faith or, seen from a

different point of view, the *sensus fidelium* or consciousness
of faith of the community, thus form an essential part of the
principle of verification of orthodoxy. Because this orthodoxy
is, as I have said, the theoretical aspect of christian praxis, the
'acclamation' or 'amen' forms an essential part of the structure
of the christian liturgy in which orthodoxy is above all to be
found: *lex orandi, lex credendi*.[49] However necessary it may
be, theology is no more than a reduction of this. It may be
called 'orthodoxy with clipped wings'.

III The church's teaching office in the functioning of these criteria

According to the catholic view, the church's teaching office
has the right and duty, in this new situation as well, to watch
over the christian character or orthodoxy (in the sense in
which I have defined it) of the faith of the church, including
her theologians. This function has not ceased to be valid
because sociological factors have nowadays given rise to a
pluralism that is qualitatively different from and more con-
fusing than the pluralism of the past. What this new situation
is bound to lead to is that the church's teaching office will
have to function in a new way, in which the deep intention
of the exercise of authority as in the early church may once
again be stressed and be borne up by the authority of authentic events, in which the christian may see the guidance of the
Holy Spirit. Authority in the church has not always been
seen in the right perspective and the true relationships have
in fact often been turned upside down. For example, the
statement is made: scripture has authority, because it is
inspired by God. From the point of view of the history of
dogma, however, the very opposite has to be affirmed: that
scripture bears authentic witness to a historical event and its
meaning, that christians certainly understand this event as
such, that they submit to this interpretation of its meaning
by scripture and therefore acknowledge the authority of scripture. Finally, after all this, they interpret this existential
authority of scripture by the statement, scripture is inspired
by God. At the beginning, then, stands not the formal
authority of scripture, but the event and the text, the
authority of which is accepted and interpreted in faith because of its significance, which makes an appeal to and is
recognised by christians. The point of departure, in other

words, is the authority of the event itself as recognised in its determining function with regard to human life. The present situation has given new scope to the expression of this fundamental view.

Pluralism does not mean that everything is now possible in the church of Christ. What is, however, increasingly clear is that the exercise of the pastoral teaching office is becoming more and more a pastoral regulation of the christian use of language, as it clearly was, for example, at Nicaea and Chalcedon.[50] This regulation, which aims to safeguard the rules of what I have already discussed above, is urgent not simply because of the matter itself (the fundamental elements of faith or the *kerygma*) but is also conditioned by historical and social factors (the structurising principles). At the moment, we are no longer moving within the same sphere of language. It is possible to formulate, in a new, orthodox manner, the dogmas of, for example, the Trinity and of Christ, without making use of the concepts 'one nature, three persons' and 'one person, two natures'. It is therefore possible for the language of the church's teaching office to be used to formulate expressions of faith that are different from those that have been in fact used in the past and this language will not be determined purely by the matter itself. The church, after all, cannot autonomously determine the development of language. Concepts like 'person' and 'nature' have come to acquire a different content from the one that they had in the early church. The attempt to preserve these concepts inherited from the past only results in the church's dogma—the christian message—becoming semantically unintelligible in the modern age. On the basis of a fairly uniform theology and philosophy, it was, in the past, somewhat easier to define dogma in the church. The real possibility of pluralism was very small and, what is more, little thought was given to it. Now, however, it is very important for the church's profession of faith and for the whole life of the christian community to arrive at a regulation of its use of language. This does not, however, apply in exactly the same way to theological reflection, which can justifiably be expressed differently from the way in which the church's statements and her liturgy are expressed, because theology also has the task of preparing the way for future preaching and liturgy. It therefore does not seem to be theologically justified, in fact, it even seems to be impossible from

the theological point of view, to try to determine theological
concepts for ever by regulating the church's language. Pronouncements, even dogmatic ones, have meaning only within
their specific contexts. Whenever they are made within a
different context, the result is always a change in the meaning of what is being affirmed. A pronouncement made at an
earlier period of history continues to be valid within its original context, which is why it is also able to point in the
direction in which the same mystery has to be expressed
within a different context.

Some christians are able to agree in principle with this
view, but insist on making a distinction between free, technically 'theological' discussion and what is called the episcopal
or hierarchical 'pedagogy of faith', a distinction which as a
believer I acknowledge in principle. It is, however, very difficult to overlook the fact that the increased extent of modern
means of communication has made this sharp distinction an
abstraction. To insist on its application is ultimately to undermine theological research and its tentative putting forward
of new interpretations with the future in mind, and to reduce
the 'pedagogy of faith' to the level of an unfair principle. I
think that it is inevitable that there will, in the future, be a
tension and indeed a certain conflict between theological
views and the views of the church's *magisterium*. This is
bound to be a normal situation in the church, if the catholic
church is not to become a mere ideology. (I do not wish to
suggest here, of course, that theologians represent 'openness'
in the church or that an inhibiting 'closedness' characterises
the hierarchical leaders of the church. The very reverse is by
no means impossible.)

It is even possible to say that the church's teaching authority is not a criterion of orthodoxy since it is itself subject to
the word of God.[51] In view of the new situation in which the
christian community is placed since the emergence of so many
different interpretations of faith, the teaching office must
above all serve as a means of communication within the community itself and guarantee an institutional freedom in which
open dialogue can take place and in which all views can be
heard. Any attempted manipulations must be prevented by
that teaching authority so that a free consensus of opinion can
come about within the community of believers.

Within this general function, the church's teaching office

has another special task. It is to establish, within the changes that are taking place in society, which language is to be regarded as valid in the church. It has, for instance, to regulate the church's use of language and make decisions in cases where someone expresses certain views concerning faith in a particular social situation with its own special historical conditions. These may perhaps endanger, if not his own faith, then that of other christians, by distorting the meaning of the reality of salvation as intended by the gospel message. The truth of faith is, of course, expressed in the church's regulation of the language of faith, but only indirectly. The intention is not to exclude all other possible expressions. Dogmas are only true in the context of the questions that they seek to answer, directly at least. They arise because the church chooses one of many different historically conditioned alternatives within a given historical situation. That situation may oblige the church to make that particular choice, with the result that other possibilities, which may, up to that moment, have been chosen, are now excluded, although there still remains a certain openness to alternatives.

In this sense, we may therefore say that dogmas certainly have a historically conditioned setting, even though their meaning continues to be relevant to us today. It is, however, left to the theologians, who will naturally respect the intention of this regulation of language by the church's teaching office, to interpret, in a justifiable way, the profession of faith that is common to all believers in the present context, in contact with the past, present and future-directed consciousness of faith of the whole community of the church. The community of believers is, after all, the bearer and the subject of theological hermeneutics. The earlier dogmas, which are the church's regulation of talk about faith in an earlier period of history, therefore continue to be our normative guide now; in their own way and at their own period, they protected christian faith and they remain the model for our own guardianship of the truth. But they are also *norma normata*; they are determined by the norm of scripture (as the first normative expression of the community of believers). They are a way, adapted to a different social and historical situation, of safeguarding what has been expressed and discussed evocatively in scripture as assertory or performative with regard to the christian community. The teaching authority of the church is an essential element of the pastoral office. It is not a 'doctrinal institution' or a 'department for truth'. The official charisma of the church must therefore be regarded as an essential charismatic help to the official proclamation which announces the good news of the gospel, and must always include this good news unreduced. This is why not only K. Rahner but also B. van Iersel were right to declare that dogmas 'regulate the use of language . . . with regard to the re-interpretation of scriptures' interpretation of reality'.[52] They do not have a direct function in connection with the interpretation of reality but, as determined by scripture, they do serve as models which direct, in faithfulness to the gospel, our theological re-interpretation of the one christian faith. This is not an insignificant task. In the re-interpretation of religious speech, what must always be taken into account is the language which was used in the past and is used now by the community of faith, the church. We cannot simply reform religious language on our own account, without asking whether others will understand our new language, because the aim of every re-interpretation and reformulation is not to make what is said more obscure, but to make it more easily understood.

The new situation places, I believe, a greater responsibility on the shoulders of theologians than they had in the past, but it also requires them to be more modest, more humble and more loving in their service of the community of believers. The scientific method used in hermeneutics and linguistic analysis must be no more than the necessary specialised equipment of a genuinely christian act of charity and *koinonia*. Otherwise the whole science of theology, with its logical, structural and phenomenological linguistic analysis and its ontological hermeneutics, will perhaps be an interesting exercise, but ultimately a non-christian undertaking. It is certainly true to say that a team of scriptural specialists and theologians can acquire more moral authority even than papal encyclicals in the catholic church. This may or may not be regretted, but as a fact it cannot be disputed. Nonetheless, it should not be an occasion of glory or of unchristian emancipation for the specialists concerned. It is certainly a sign that the situation has changed and, in my opinion, contains above all a warning to theologians not to play the pope in their own way; to avoid incurring the justified criticism that has been made of some of those who have in the past held the office of Peter in the church, to avoid the heresy of their own orthodoxy. The criticism that I have outlined concerning theologians' 'own' orthodoxy applies equally well to the claim made by our own contemporary theological understanding of faith. 'Patient dialogue, even if it seems hopeless, is a more real experience of being a church on the way than either excommunication or leaving' the church or one's office.[53] Quite apart from all political or strategic motives, this is a truly humanising expression of human and christian criticism of ideology as an ecclesial service to the world.

5
CORRELATION BETWEEN HUMAN
QUESTION AND CHRISTIAN ANSWER

For a long time, one of the basic themes in ecumenical dialogue has been that of natural theology and, closely connected with this, the problem of the correlation between the human question and the answer given by revelation towards which either a negative or a positive attitude has been taken. I shall call this 'the question-answer correlation'. As a result of the hermeneutic problem, there has been a remarkable change recently in the significance of this theme. When a problem changes, the questions which result from it also change. To begin with, then, I should like to clarify these two concepts: the 'problem' and the 'resulting question'.

By 'problem', in this context, I mean the formation of a theory determined by social factors, for infrastructures can also cause truth to arise. There is a dialectical relationship between the social infrastructure and our valid insights in the field of philosophy, theology and religion. In this light, a 'problem' can be described as a totality of social and historical circumstances which cause a given human community to ask certain questions, questions which were not asked in a different period or situation. Obviously, a clearly defined historical configuration, a definite way of associating with the world, of interpreting, reacting and so on, correspond to a definite question. In this sense it can be said that a problem arises from the pressures of the historically conditioned situation. This problem is not freely chosen and cannot therefore be avoided or ignored with an easy conscience. We are, on the

contrary, obviously forced, in view of the actual situation and
its infrastructure, to take up an attitude towards it. In this
sense, we are all men of our own time—of a period which
forces us to ask certain questions which were not asked in the
past because the time was not ripe for them.

A problem is therefore historically conditioned and, in this
sense, changeable. Every period of history has its own problem. If the problem is changed, the resulting question cannot
be answered, at least directly, with the earlier answer. What
is more, the earlier question cannot be asked outside its own
problem without at least partially changing the meaning of it.

In the controversial theology of the past, the problem of
the question-answer-correlation was whether man could, in
principle, meaningfully prove the existence of God entirely
through his own resources and therefore without the help of
God's revelation. Until the time of the enlightenment, however, this question was asked, both by protestant and by
catholic theologians, within a social framework in which, in
one way or another, the existence of God was to a great extent accepted. Now, on the other hand, we live at a time and
in a society which are 'secular' and the problem is therefore
quite differently situated. Before attempting to answer the
question of whether the way can be opened rationally to the
mystery of God, we must first examine whether the question
itself is still meaningful. This is no longer taken simply for
granted, as it was in the past. Is this question, precisely as a
question, still meaningful or intelligible in a world which has
been subjected to the criticism of religion made by such
thinkers as Feuerbach, Marx, Freud, Marcuse and, at least
indirectly, Einstein? If, in the light of what I have said, the
old question were reformulated, it would have to be expressed
in the following way: is it possible meaningfully to prove
the existence of God from the standpoint of an atheistic,
secular interpretation of the world? Expressed in this way,
the question would of course be meaningless

I Reformulation of the question of God

A new question has arisen from the new problem. This can
be formulated in the following way: is the question of God
a serious one, is it really meaningful, and if so under what
conditions is it meaningful? What is at issue, then, is whether
it is meaningful and justified even to put the question of

God. Under what conditions can a religious attitude and faith in christian revelation avoid the criticism that it is a mystification, a projection of man's mind? What is the condition of understanding christian revelation?

The questions which arise here have a far-reaching significance. Whether christianity can do anything else in the present situation other than protest against the complete secularisation of the modern world and, what is more, do this simply by bearing witness, without any possibility of entering into real dialogue with this non-christian world, depends on the answer that is given to these questions. Talk about God has, admittedly, found itself in a dilemma. Either christians claim to have a monopoly of being able to talk meaningfully about God, with the result that only christian talk about God is, in their opinion, meaningful, and this too only on the basis of subjective conviction, or the criticism of theism also applies to christian talk about God, which would be the end of all theology. If all forms of natural theology are denied, it seems as though, between man's questions about human significance on the one hand and the religious attitude on the other, a division of such magnitude arises that all religion must ultimately appear to be unjustified and unintelligible to human experience.

This modern challenge to christianity has been expressed by Heidegger as follows: 'Anyone who has experienced theology, both that of the christian faith and that of philosophy, from its origins prefers now to be silent about God in the sphere of thought'.[54] Karl Barth clearly chose one of the courses in the dilemma when, at least initially, he affirmed that all talk about God was a christian privilege, and the still pugnacious theologian H. Gollwitzer supports him in this.[55] This position is very difficult to maintain, however, since this christian talk about God has recently been attacked by such theologians as Paul van Buren and Herbert Braun and by many others who follow the tradition of linguistic analysis. They ask christians pertinently enough to legitimate our faith in God, that is, to make it cognitively significant. The christian, in other words, is no longer able to withdraw into an area free from criticism, where he can forbid the entry of human thought and scientific and critical questions.

The result of this situation is that the question-answer-correlation has been debated in a new way in christian theology—by the later Barth and by Brunner, Bultmann, Tillich, Ebeling, Gogarten, Pannenberg and Moltmann, to name only a few of the more prominent theologians. Tillich especially has given an important place in his *Systematic Theology* to this question. For each particular theme as well as for christianity as a whole he relates the christian answer to man's existential question: to the question which man himself is. Unlike Barth and Bultmann, Tillich avoids deducing this question that is identical with human existence from the answer by revelation.[56] If christian revelation does not provide an answer to a question which precedes and is asked quite independently of revelation, then this answer will inevitably be unintelligible and be experienced as meaningless. The question-answer-correlation aims to show that christian talk about God is not non-obligatory, but binding and therefore universally valid. It can only be accepted as true if the expression of the truth of the christian message provides an adequate answer for the present generation. Ebeling also affirms that christian talk about God concerns all men and has therefore to be made intelligible to all men.[57] Theology establishes the binding character of its talk about God by stating explicitly that it is an answer to the question of man's existence.

This tendency can also be discerned elsewhere where the present-day problem of the question-answer-correlation is discussed. The correlation between question and answer has come to occupy a central place in protestant theology today and this has meant that the intelligibility and above all the universal validity of christianity and of christian talk about God are explicitly debated. I am of the opinion that this is an attempt to overcome the rather one-sided 'fideism' which was emphasised in the earlier theology of the reformation and which tended to lead to a fundamental division between the church and the world. The historical situation in which christianity is placed today certainly impels theologians to try to bridge this gap. In this, protestant theology is very close to catholic theology, in which a similar problem is at present being debated with renewed interest in the proofs of the existence of God, which have to be approached in a new way because of the changed situation.

The underlying intention in catholic and protestant theology is clearly this. Protestant and catholic theologians are both looking for the human, existential and social relevance of the christian affirmation of God as an answer to the question which is asked of christians: 'What difference does it make to me whether I believe in God or not?'. The question which inevitably accompanies this first question is: 'What use is it to me? Does it do or mean anything to me?'. The fact that relevance and intelligibility are historically conditioned and not an absolute norm, and that the question of reality goes more deeply than this historically conditioned question concerning meaning is usually not ignored. On the other hand, however, it is impossible not to recognise that, if the question of meaning is not answered, man remains inaccessible to possible signs of transcendence in human experience and will not ask himself the real question of truth and reality. The function of truth is, after all, to liberate man. Modern secularised man is, moreover, very afraid of venerating what is not worth venerating The dilemma may therefore be formulated in the following way. On the one hand, christian talk about God may not present itself as something that makes man's ability and knowledge within the world fruitful and successful, because faith in God is not a guarantee against the risks that we encounter here on earth and does not lessen in any way the vertigo caused by being men in an ambivalent history. On the other hand, faith must have something to offer which is humanly and meaningfully relevant, within the context of our experience, to our being as men.

All the christian churches are looking for the exact solution which will do justice to both sides of the dilemma and, in this search, what is being especially discussed is how it is possible to arrive at the real pre-understanding and the true sphere of understanding for the exegesis and proclamation of the biblical witness to God's activity. In this context, Gerhard Ebeling has said: 'The understanding of what is meant by the word "God" has its place in the sphere of the radical question which man is'.[58] This quotation is certainly very reminiscent of catholic natural theology and is really very little different from the conclusion which Thomas Aquinas reached at the end of his *quinque viae*. Within a christian social context, he took as his point of departure the question raised by the world and postulated the need for an 'all-supporting ground', for a non-christian pre-understand-

ing. He identified this all-supporting ground with God, but
this was not a conclusion of his proof of the existence of God,
it was a profession of christian faith. From rational argument,
he concluded not to *ergo Deus existit,* but to *et hoc omnes
dicunt Deum.* In other words, as a believer, he identified the
end of his philosophical analysis, which led him from the
empirical phenomena of human experience to an all-supporting point of reference, with the living God. This identification was not a philosophical transition, but a transition
made in faith: Thomas indicated the point where christian
talk about God becomes intelligible within the context of
human experience, at least in medieval times.

The ecumenical situation now is quite different from what
it was in the past. Both catholic and protestant theology now
lead to what is practically the same question. The christian
answer to the question of what the christian religion means
by 'God' can only be made intelligible if it is related to the
radical and necessary question which man is himself. Theologians are therefore looking for something in our human life
which will make what christians mean by 'God' intelligible,
so that it can be seen that what the christian churches are
saying about the old and new testaments is not the monopoly
of an exclusive club which has no message for the rest of the
world, but which is precisely a message for all people. The
hermeneutic problem of making the christian revelation intelligible, of presenting an interpretation of reality which can
be called 'theistic' (quite apart from the historical overtones
contained in this word) is without doubt a question of life
and death for christianity. We have to be 'prepared to make a
defence ... for the hope that is in us' (1 Pet 3:15). In our
modern world, which is so free as far as faith is concerned,
it is not only an honour, but also a duty for a christian, and
especially for a christian theologian, to make what we mean
when we speak about God intelligible and meaningful to all
men. This hermeneutic tendency, then, is not really directed
towards proving the existence of God, but towards making
the christian revelation intelligible. Since the enlightenment,
however, faith in God (and gods) has no longer been taken
for granted, and for this reason the question of the human
context within which God can be meaningfully discussed has
become extremely urgent. In the presence of a secularised
world, for which God is a 'useless hypothesis', protestantism

and catholicism are joining forces in their reflection on a natural theology.

II Problems involved in the correlation

So far, then, the prospect seems favourable; the problem of the question-answer-correlation appears not only to have a meaningful place in christian thought, but also to be regarded as extremely urgent by all the churches. Several very difficult problems, however, are involved in this, some of which have already been recognised by the theologians whom I have mentioned. Although they reveal important mutual differences, the later Barth, Brunner, Bultmann, Ebeling, Tillich, Gogarten and Moltmann have all affirmed that a certain independence has to be accorded to man's question about God, but that the real and full purport of this question can only be formulated theologically; in other words the question itself only becomes clear in the light of the answer provided by christian revelation. It looks as though the real intention has been by-passed in this way. If man's question about himself can only be identified by christianity as a question concerning God, then the universal validity of christianity can hardly be demonstrated on the basis of the question-answer-correlation. Yet this was the original intention of this theology of correlation. It is possible and also quite correct to affirm that only God can speak meaningfully about God, but the difficulty here is that the word 'God' means nothing to a very large section of contemporary mankind, and a God who means nothing can hardly be experienced in and through the christian revelation as meaning something that can be called relevant.

Here, the intelligibility—not, I would stress, the rationality —of the christian mystery is really at stake. What depends on the solution to this difficulty is whether or not christianity can still carry out a mission in the modern world. If only God can speak meaningfully about God, the door is, paradoxically enough, at once opened to the atheistic criticism of religion, because God's speaking about himself reaches us only in human words, since this is the only way for it to be intelligible to us. But these human words would have to express the transcendent, the inexpressible, the *Deus quo magis cogitari nequit,* and they would therefore be defenceless against the criticism of philosophy. We should then have to admit

that the 'death of God' theologians were right to assert that
the only possibly justified way of speaking about God is to
remain silent about him. This then, would seem to be
rationally justified, but however much this 'negative theology' may express something that is essential in christianity,
we cannot be completely silent about God. The problem
cannot be suppressed therefore: we have at least to speak
of our silence about God.

This is, however, not the whole of the difficulty. The correlative method also encounters difficulties from quite a different quarter, from linguistic analysis. A fundamental question
posed by the linguistic analysts is whether a religious answer
can be given to a non-religious question. In this case, the
linguistic analysts would ask: is not the question in a different
language game from the answer? A 'category mistake' of this
kind is the very definition of meaninglessness for the linguistic analyst. If the answer given to the question 'is the world
a globe?' is 'it is very beautiful', this is not an untruth, but
it is, on the other hand, not an answer to the question. In
this context, the answer is meaningless. We have therefore to
ask ourselves whether it is meaningful to give a theological
answer to a philosophical question. A similar confusion certainly does occur, for example, in dialogue between psycho-
logists, sociologists and theologians. The question asked by a
psychologist from his own, psychological pattern of interpretation cannot be answered meaningfully by a theologian if
he remains within his own, theological pattern of interpretation. Nonetheless, theologians do try to do this, or otherwise
the only answers they give to psychological and sociological
questions are a hotchpotch of theological insights and snip-
pets of psychological and sociological knowledge. Paul Tillich
above all recognised this danger, although it is probably true
to say that he was only implicitly aware of it and did not
formulate it explicitly. In any case, he did certainly formulate anew the philosophical question theologically in the
light of the christian answer. This of course undermines the
intention of the correlative method, because the answer to
such a re-formulated question is only valid for the christian and
is not universally valid: it is not a truth that binds all men.
It therefore looks as though, if the question is asked philo-
sophically, the answer must also be given within the philosophical language game, if it is to be universally meaningful.

God, an essentially religious reality, can therefore not be the answer to a non-religious question. In that case, how can the correlative method still be relevant? Linguistic analysis thus puts a spoke in the wheel. And even if linguistic analysis is unable to help us to solve the question of truth, it does in my opinion have something useful to say about the question of meaning and correlation. The question of meaning is connected with that of truth, but they are not identical. From the point of view of phenomenology and linguistic analysis, the question of meaning precedes the question of truth: only a meaningful statement can be true or false and a meaningless affirmation is neither true nor false. (Husserl and Wittgenstein are in agreement with each other here.)

According to the later Wittgenstein and to Ian T. Ramsey, who bases his ideas on Wittgenstein, the religious context is the only language game within which the word 'God' has a meaningful place, and speaking about God is therefore humanly intelligible. It is only within the whole of religious activity that talk about God acquires a clearly defined, intelligible meaning. Internal criteria of meaning can therefore be constructed for it. Thus christian talk about God is different, for example, from buddhist talk about God. Outside the purely religious context—in the sphere of the empirical sciences, for example—talk about God as such is simply meaningless, seen from the point of view of linguistic analysis. The opposite is also true: talk about God can, as such, never be empirical or purely descriptive. The real context within which the christian speaks about God, then, is that of the life, death and resurrection of the man Jesus, acknowledged to be the Christ, the one who is the living prototype of and determines the ultimate meaning of our human life and history, seen against the background of old testament religion which was itself a differentiation from the varied religions prevalent in the ancient Near East. The linguistic analysts, especially those who deny the meaningful character of a meta-language (that is a statement made about a statement from a different language game) maintain that christian talk about God is only meaningful and intelligible to those who are inwardly involved in this language game. Christians therefore confront non-christians with empty hands, saying 'we can see what you cannot see'.

If the correlative method is approached from the standpoint of linguistic analysis, then, there are very great obstacles, especially in connection with the christian mission to the world. If talk about God is only meaningful in a religious context, this word 'God' is by definition unintelligible to non-believers and it is consequently pointless for them to listen to christian preaching, because this religious language game is alien to them.

A frequent answer given particularly by protestant theologians to this difficulty is that the christian revelation brings with it its own intelligibility: it brings about a conversion in man. But we are bound to ask how this transition from meaninglessness to meaningfulness comes about. The answer to this question is not the operation of God's grace, because it is necessary for the convert to perform by grace a humanly justified, meaningful action. It is clear enough that a man would not turn to God for purely intellectual reasons but, in that case, do we have to affirm, together with the dialectical theologians, that man comes to God precisely in order to overcome the meaninglessness of his life? The linguistic analysts, on the other hand, take completely the opposite point of view and maintain, on the basis of what we are bound to recognise as a real experience, that speaking about man and the world is meaningful and intelligible to modern man, but that speaking about God is, on the contrary, meaningless to anyone who has not, or has not yet, found his place in the religious language game.

Dialectical theology thus came into violent conflict with the present-day world. This has resulted in christian theologians becoming rather wary of dialectical theology and gradually but radically reacting against it. They are, it would seem, tending to dissociate themselves from the theology both of Barth and of Bultmann. The real contribution made by dialectical theology should not be underestimated, but both the Barthian and the Bultmannian versions of this theology do have the disadvantage of placing such strong emphasis on the transcendent reality of God, the 'wholly other', that faith has become an unintelligible decision and the factual discrepancy between faith and the context of man's experience has been almost canonised. The universal claim of faith was, it is true, affirmed, but it was also in principle undermined. As a result, christianity became, within the society in which man lives, a sphere of close security without the critical

strength which could result in a real liberation of man in his
history on this earth. It is easy to see now that the logical
and historical consequence of this theology had, sooner or
later, to be the 'death of God' theology, which was exclusively
concerned with the uniqueness of the man Jesus and at the
same time re-affirmed the critical strength of this view of Jesus
with regard to the social activity of the christian in the world.
In this way, prominence was given to an aspect of truth
which had been neglected by Barth and Bultmann, but the
scales were tipped too much in the other direction. Because
the distinctive character of Jesus was separated from his
unique relationship with God, christianity became simply
one among other religious phenomena without any claim to
universality. This misunderstanding of the distinctive character of Jesus—if one fails to express this relationship with
God—means that christianity can simply be overlooked as a
critical force which can liberate man. This seems to me at
least to be the result with which we are confronted at the
moment.

For a very long time, catholic theologians looked for a
purely metaphysically orientated 'natural theology', which
tried to attribute meaning to God before he began to
speak. This theology also failed through its unintelligibility,
precisely because of its rigid and abstractly metaphysical standpoint. Present-day catholic theologians are tending to dissociate themselves from this earlier theology. It is, after all,
meaningless to let the question of the truth of religious
statements precede the question of their meaning. The
christian does not believe in an unintelligible hocus-pocus,
but in a mystery that is meaningful. How could anyone feel
that he was being personally addressed by the mystery proclaimed to him if the meaning of that mystery were not to
some extent accessible to him? The question of meaning
logically precedes that of truth, and a statement only has
meaning if in one way or another it expresses lived experience.

The missionary task of christianity and the transition from
non-christian to christian thus confront us with the need for
an explicitly non-religious context of experience within which
it is possible to listen meaningfully to christian talk about
God in a secularised world, Even theology itself can be seen
as the limit of meaningful talk about God. It is meaningful
because it belongs to the whole of the religious language

game and it is the limit because it is as such a scientific undertaking, a critical reflection on christian revelation and a meaningful formulation and actualisation of that revelation. We
can, however, ask whether theology is really the farthest limit
of meaningful talk about God. Perhaps we must regard man
himself as this farthest limit and have therefore to turn to
philosophy, where in that case there could and should be
meaningful talk about God outside the christian revelation.

Philosophy can in fact tell us how believers, assuming
therefore their faith in God, must speak meaningfully about
God, because it makes a distinction between the different
language games and investigates their structures and their
mutual relationships. It considers the possibility and the
conditions of human behaviour and therefore also the possibility and the conditions of human speech, including christian
talk about God. Assuming this religious talk about God, it
can therefore show where this talk can find a place in human
language which will make it meaningful. In this sense, theology is, I believe, really subject to the criticism of philosophy,
which verifies the logical status, the meaningfulness and the
intelligibility of our theological talk. Philosophy can demonstrate that talk about God is at the limit of all meaningful
speech and that it is to be found where language becomes
speechless and therefore reaches a limit, but also speaks about
the limit of man in his world. Philosophy itself cannot fill
this speechless space—only religion, the believer, can do that
—but it can certainly show where religious talk has a meaningful place in our world and our experience. What is more,
it is clear from this that every religious statement about God
will at the same time be a statement about man and his
world. It is in this way that the secular interpretation of
christianity is to be understood and it is only in that sense
that I would go along with this interpretation. Because man
is conditioned by history, our talk about God will inevitably
bear traces of our human history.

It is only if we give a place in our theological reflection to
these critical questions of philosophy about the meaningfulness and intelligibility of religious talk in general, with its
theological, dogmatic, liturgical and confessional aspects, that
the distinctive element of christian talk about God will become apparent. It will then become apparent that the theologians whom I have mentioned as concerned with the

correlation between question and answer are really mis-
judging the authentic correlation and thus defeat their object.
In the first place, only a human answer is correlative to a
human question: only man can answer meaningfully a
question which he himself asks before he can understand a
possibly transcendent, divine word of revelation. Christianity
cannot answer a human question directly; to do this would
be to make, from the point of view of linguistic analysis, a
category mistake, by breaking through the question-answer-
correlation and showing a lack of understanding of both the
human question and the transcendent christian answer. A
true question is always directed towards something, to
some extent it anticipates the answer. We are not concerned
here with a question which has no content and to which no
answer is expected. If we do not solve the difficulties connected with this question about ourselves, then we must expect the legitimate criticism of the humanists and atheists,
namely that our God is a 'stop-gap', something to which you
resort if you can find no other way out of your deepest
problems. This criticism in any case impels us to investigate
how man himself can solve his problem. If an answer can be
found to this question, christian revelation can then present
itself as an unexpected, surprising and gratuitous answer
which completely transcends the question itself. It would then
not only make the question itself clearer and deeper, as the
theologians of the correlative method claim, but would probably also leave the question entirely behind and perhaps subject it to questioning. We shall, in other words, only be able
to worship God properly when we no longer need him in any
way to solve or to minimise our existential and social problem.
It is only then that God can be worthy of our worship and
that *agape* can clearly become happiness as a gift that is
purely without necessity, as when a hostess says to a visitor
who hands her flowers, although she is happy and grateful,
'it really was not necessary'. Authentic human life seems un-
thinkable unless we experience complete gratuity. Is this perhaps the authentic correlation between our being men and
God's grace? In this sense, unnecessary, useless and gratuitous
liturgy, worship and praise of God becomes completely meaningful, while it is in itself meaningless to modern man who
has 'come of age' because it is not, or at least not directly,
functional for the world and human society.

III Indirect experience of the universal validity of christian talk about God

Our question, then, is this: where can the problem posed by man himself find a meaningful human answer which precedes the explicitly christian answer and which, even though this answer may be impotent and faltering, is directly related to real human questions? How too are we to come from this point to the point where a justified method of correlation can be formulated? To put it another way, what does the universal pre-understanding consist of—that universal understanding without which the christian message cannot be universally valid?

I believe that it is possible to formulate such a new method of correlation and, in this method, I should like to distinguish two basic aspects: on the one hand, 'critical negativity' or negative dialectics and, on the other, a positive sphere of meaning and factual, particular experiences of meaningfulness.

A. NEGATIVE DIALECTICS

Man's quest for meaning is in fact answered in many different ways. This has resulted in a pluriformity of positive views of man which are not, as such, representative of mankind as a whole and cannot therefore form the basis for the universal claim of the christian answer. If we were to confine ourselves purely to this dimension of reality, theology would become little more than a fashionable imitation of the contemporary way of life. Any serious method of correlation is bound to fail if it does not preserve the critical distance that we learn to acquire especially by remembering the past with a better future in mind. Without this critical distance, the present functions as an uncriticised pre-decision with regard to the christian faith.

All the same, it is possible to distinguish, in all these human answers to man's deepest question about meaning, something that is common to all of them and therefore universal. This is, however, negative, although it is clearly sustained by an unexpressed positive sphere of meaning. Despite all pluralism, then, there is, in positive views of man, the element of a common search to realise the constantly threatened *humanum*. It is impossible to formulate the positive content of this *humanum* without reverting to many different, fragmentary and mutually contradictory views. There is, however, at least this one common basis in all these different views of man: resistance to the threat to humanity. This critical negativity, or negative dialectics, is the universal pre-understanding of all positive views of man. It is not really in the first place knowledge, but a praxis which is motivated by hope and within which an element of knowledge that can be formulated in a theory is discernible. There is, among men, a critical solidarity over the threat to humanity. There is no question here of a vague ideal of humanity. The *humanum* that is sought only becomes a universally recognised value via a negative and indirect mediation, that is, via a resistance to the inhumane. All resistance to inhumane situations reveals, if only indirectly, at least an obscure consciousness of what must be confessed positively by human integrity; it manifests in a negative and indirect way the call of and to the *humanum*. As soon as this humane element is positively articulated, either theoretically or practically in a definite plan of action, a great many theoretical and practical projects come about at once. I regard these negative dialectics coming within a positive sphere of meaning which is, however, in its universality only implicit (it is a call to the *humanum*) as the universal pre-understanding not only of the pluralist answers that man gives to this call, but also of christian talk about God, in other words, of the gospel. In a pluralist society such as ours, these negative dialectics must be seen as a critical resistance to the threat to the *humanum*, without being able to define this *humanum*, the form in which a universal experience is mediated. If this is taken as the point of departure, the christian message does not, in order to be understood, need first to place itself at the mercy of one definite philosophy or one definite image of man out of all the philosophies or views of man that we know.

In view of the fact that all positive images of man, both theoretical and practical, can be broken up into many different and mutually contradictory views and plans of action, the christian message or *kerygma* can only be geared to what is common to all—an unceasing resistance to the inhumane and a permanent search for the humane, a search that man himself tries to solve in the praxis of his life (even though this often results in inhumane behaviour). Christian identity has to do with human integrity, and even though the latter cannot be theoretically and practically defined in one all-embracing system, man's existential problem is, in it, inwardly linked with the christian revelation. Universal resistance to alienation, inhumanity and the absence of freedom assumes, in christianity, the form of a redemption by God which can be realised in and through the faith of people in history. The christian answer is at one with man's universal protest against the inhumane, but at the same time christian faith refuses to postulate a secular or universal subject of history, in other words, to point, either theoretically or practically, to a secular principle which would give unity to man's history of emancipation. The christian answer reminds man that such a universal subject of history, which everyone is seeking, really exists, but cannot be given from history itself. Neither the human individual, nor the community nor any part of society, but only the living God is recognised in christian faith (man's answer to Jesus Christ) as the universal subject of history. This is why the christian answer views very critically all theories and plans of action which postulate a positive principle of unity within and from history. A theoretical or practical system of unity of this kind potentially leads to the totalitarian rule of one man or group over other men. This is why I regard the fact that the christian answer is geared to the universally human pre-understanding as a critical solidarity with man's resistance to the inhumane. This resistance to what is inhumane, negative dialectics, which can also be found in the christian answer, is at the same time a resistance to any secular, theoretical or practical, system of unity and this is so on the basis of God's promise that has been revealed in the resurrection from man's ultimate impotence, death. A life without alienation, a realm of freedom without injustice, really is the prospect before us and exists already as a positive possibility (see 2 Pet 3 : 13; Rev 21 : 4). But even christians can only formulate this future in a negative way, in the form of a contrast. No definite plan of action has been given to them in revelation. The answer is a promise and at the same time it is critically negative.

This, then, prevents the principle of correlation of critical resistance as a universal pre-understanding of christianity from being misused. This is a real danger. In the name of and appealing to 'the threat to the *humanum*', men in history have themselves often been a threat to the *humanum*. A very striking example of this is, of course, nazism in Germany, but there have been several modern theories claiming to protect the *humanum* which have in fact resulted in a degradation of humanity. Christian faith resists any premature identification of the *humanum*. In its resistance and its protest, which is joined to the universally human protest, christianity remains critical and insists that it cannot accept any uniform positive definition of the *humanum*. The power to realise this *humanum* and to bring about an individual and collective peace is reserved for God, the power of love. This is the 'eschatological reservation'.

Individually and collectively, man needs emancipation and redemption. However this may be formulated and however inhumanly it may sometimes be expressed, this is undoubtedly man's deepest experience. The answer which christianity gives to this deepest human need is this: it is right to look for man's emancipation and, what is more, this emancipation is a positive possibility as the grace of God which has to be given definite form in history, a form which is peace, justice and love.

Christian talk about God is therefore only negatively and indirectly open to universal understanding and acceptance, in other words, it takes place via the experience that the *humanum* is always threatened, perhaps above all by its premature positive identification. To the question of the meaning that is contained within the radical historical question that man himself is, man himself gives a practical answer: on the one hand, resistance to the inhumane, though this, on the other hand, often causes the *humanum* to be even further degraded through false identification. On the basis of a more accurate analysis, this could be extended to a satisfactory method of correlation. Such a method would not give a religious or theological answer to a non-religious or philosophical question. It would also indicate the context of human experience in which christian talk about God can be heard in a way which is both secularly meaningful and universally intelligible. There is indeed a convergence or correlation between what is affirmed in the gospel message as a promise, a demand and a criticism and what man experiences as emancipation in his resistance to the threat to the *humanum* that he is seeking. The christian message gives a counter-answer containing a promise and a criticism to the living praxis of mankind insofar as man is seeking an inner and a social *shalom* or peace. Whether this christian answer is accepted or rejected, it cannot be denied that it is, as an answer in the form of promise, possibility, perspective, strength and criticism, historically relevant and meaningful to any man who is seeking the meaning of human life, whether individually or collectively, personally or politically and socially. In this way, the christian message can be made intelligible. All the same, these negative dialectics need to be supplemented.

B. POSITIVE MEANINGFUL EXPERIENCES

Because man experiences so much that is meaningless in his own life, in society and even in the churches, it is quite impossible for him to be reconciled with his fate, with his fellow-men and with society as a whole. It is only possible for him to be fully reconciled with the whole of reality, that is, to be in a state of justification, when meaningfulness and meaninglessness are no longer insanely interwoven and when fully realised meaning is actively experienced. This situation can be described as 'salvation', being whole. It can also be called the *eschaton* or perfect fulfilment of meaning without any threat, and *shalom* or eschatological peace stimulating us to establish peace here and now in our history.

We cannot simply stand still once we have accepted negative dialectics. It is even possible to say that this critical negativity is impossible and unintelligible without the justified trust that perfect meaningfulness and an experience of this meaningfulness is not entirely beyond our reach. As the 'believing atheist', Ernst Bloch, has rightly said, an 'objective hope' which makes subjective hope possible must correspond to the subjective hope which expresses itself negatively in resistance to every threat to the *humanum*. There can be no doubt that the incomplete character of our being as men as such imposes on us the task of constantly transcending ourselves. But can this incomplete character itself be, as some scholars claim, the basis which makes this transcendence of self possible and which will even bring it about? Cannot the history of men fail? Indeed, there is no need to look very far around us in the world to discover that men do make history fail.

Man can certainly avoid the question concerning the ultimate meaning of being man theoretically, that is in thought, but he cannot avoid it in action. He has in fact already answered this question in his human praxis, in a positive or a negative sense or by a nihilistic or sceptical attitude to life. He acts in the conviction that life itself is or is not worth living. In this, an important part is played by the datum of evil, the datum of what is, from the human point of view, meaningless. Evil has clearly been a datum of such great proportions in human history that neither man nor society can offer us any guarantee at all that we shall ever be able to overcome it. I was at one time rather struck by the pessimistic analyses made by Jean Nabert, a basically optimistic philosopher and the scholar under whom Paul Ricoeur studied. In his *Essai sur le mal*,[59] he tried to provide a fully sustained, critical and rational analysis of meaninglessness as realised by man. In this work, his attitude was that of a believing philosopher, but one who would not easily be suspected, in a philosophical impasse, of referring to the mystery of God. All the same, this scholar, who had a very high appreciation of ethics and wrote, among other things, a work on fundamental ethics,[60] was undeniably pessimistic about man's ethical powers and came to the conclusion that man's impotence to overcome meaninglessness and to realise meaning in human history is so great that, at this point, even ethics completely loses heart. He did not finally conclude from this that there must ultimately be a transcendent meaning, a forgiving God who overcomes all our meaninglessness, but he did postulate that, if there are, in our human society, religious traditions—such as the Jewish and the christian tradition—which speak about a revelation and a God who ultimately creates meaning and is therefore forgiving, every thinking man is bound even *a priori* to listen 'with great veneration' to that message. For, he argued, it is clear from human history that this real problem of meaninglessness in life and society cannot be solved rationally or ethically, theoretically or practically, by man himself.

All the same, I think that it is necessary to go further than Nabert has gone. It seems to me undeniable that human life includes particular experiences which are signs or glimpses of an ultimate total meaning of human life. All our negative experiences cannot brush aside the 'nonetheless' of the trust which is revealed in man's critical resistance and which prevents us from simply surrendering man, human society and the world entirely to total meaninglessness. This trust in the ultimate meaning of human life seems to me to be the basic presupposition of man's action in history.

The dialectical theologians rightly regard the figure of Christ as the simultaneous revelation of the meaninglessness of man's life and of the unmerited meaningfulness of what is offered to him in Christ. One has the impression sometimes, however, that the meaninglessness and the non-goodness of the world is approached precisely in order to make it clear that all meaning and goodness can be expected only from Christ. In this way, a fact of human experience is completely overlooked, namely that non-believers are also committed to the task of improving the world and of overcoming all meaninglessness in the world. This tendency has been rightly criticised, from the point of view of the christian faith in creation, by the lutheran theologian K. Logstrup.[61] It is difficult to regard it as meaningful that silence should first be preserved about God's creative activity and then, after the meaninglessness of human history has been established, a place should be given to the christian faith in creation, as an aspect of the doctrine of redemption. It is certainly the task of theology to clarify the radical limitation and sinfulness of human existence to its structures, but it is equally the task of theology to illuminate the implications of the goodness which is due to the world originally on the basis of creation. The antimetaphysical tendency that is prevalent in contemporary catholic and protestant theology seems to be traceable to the fear that, if christian faith has lines of communication with a rational human insight into reality and does not form an 'untouchable area' within it, it would be based on data which man can have at his disposal, with the result that revelation would no longer be an 'event' or *Er-eignis* in the Bultmannian sense of something which takes possession of man (*eigen*, own). In reasoning in this way, however, there is a tendency to forget that there are also, at the level of the world, things which are 'given', but which are not for this reason 'available' or 'at man's disposal' in Bultmann's sense of *verfügbar*. One has only to think, in this context, of friendship, love, personal encounters and fidelity in marriage, for example. All these and similar realities clearly have the character of an 'event' in the Bultmannian sense. They cannot be completely functionalised, we cannot take possession of them, but they take possession of us. They are, moreover, not purely human projections, as is evident from the recognition of the personal dignity of our fellow-men which is contained in them. These human realities are sustained by a gratuitous meaning in itself, which communicates itself to us in them and takes possession of us.

It is therefore both possible and meaningful to regard, even apart from revelation, human life as more than simply meaninglessness, but as a manifestation of essential goodness, even if this manifestation is often impotent. In this consideration of reality from the point of view of man's question about the authentic fulfilment of his life, about salvation, I see the only explicitly non-religious context within which it is meaningful to speak correlatively about God according to the criteria of the religious language game. It is certainly not meaningful to give a religious answer to a non-religious question, because, in this case, question and answer belong to two different language games and, according to the rules of linguistic analysis, a 'category mistake' is committed. We can only say that this takes place in the case outlined above, however, if we lose sight of the profundity of our human existence—our being an *Ereignis* or 'event' in the Bultmannian sense. Man's question concerning himself, which is apparently not a religious question, is in fact sustained by the reality of creation and is thus, implicitly, rooted in the soil of all religious experience: God's sovereign and unexpected act of creation which is not overcome by our sinfulness. The superior power of God's good act of creation arouses in us the quest for the real basis of the datum of experience that people, despite everything (and often without knowing about the redemption of Christ) continue their trust that goodness and not evil must have the last word. The christian revelation extends this 'must have' to 'will have'; but without man's 'must have', the christian 'will have' would be unintelligible. The ultimate fulfilment of man at the end of time, which all men are seeking but cannot formulate and can only partly realise, is the universal pre-understanding of the *humanum* that is promised to us in Christ. Eschatology and christology coincide essentially here. Human reality, which can, despite everything, be meaningfully interpreted in secular terms and especially by realising meaning in praxis within a history of meaninglessness, receives from christianity meaning in abundance: the living God himself, who is ultimately the abundance to which all secular meaning is indebted for its own secular significance.

I have not, of course, penetrated to the deepest mystery of the christian message itself in this argument, but have remained at the threshold with man himself, for whom christian talk about God must be intelligible. I should have preferred to speak about christianity itself, but I believe that the first task of christians today is to listen very attentively to the world in order to collect the material with which they will be able to make christianity accessible to their fellow-men, because it is precisely here that the greatest unsolved problems are still to be found. We cannot avoid analysing man's alienations more fully and exposing the dimension in our humanity in which christian talk about God can be intelligible. What is more, this does not exclude the fact that it will also imply a self-denying *metanoia* on man's part to listen. Christian talk about God will not be accessible to contemporary man if he does not experience, in his actual life, signs and glimpses of transcendence, and does not come to understand that an exclusively scientific and technological interpretation of reality inevitably leads to many forms of inhumanity. It is true that man will not at once experience the space which is made free, after these alienations have been analysed, as a question about God, but it does, on the other hand, seem as if only this context of human experience offers a sensitive point of resonance for christian talk about God, which can only there be meaningful and intelligible as good news. We can in fact dispense less now than in the past with a natural theology faithful to human experience.

I would personally not maintain that the question-answer-correlation, seen as the pre-understanding of christianity and the basis of its universal validity, could be interpreted as man asking a question and christian revelation being the answer to this question. This does not, in my view, make revelation intelligible; it would be playing, as it were, according to the rules of two different language games at the same time. I would rather formulate the correlation in this way: man, who, despite everything, is looking for meaning in the world, asks a question and he must first answer this question himself. Something of the wonder of man's existence which he is trying, despite everything, to realise and which he, despite Dachau, Buchenwald and Vietnam, and despite the hidden

personal, spiritual and social misery of so many of his fellow-
men, continues to trust in and commit himself to, believing
that good will prevail, can be discerned in this human
answer. What can, in fact, be observed in very many men is
that there is something in man that does not come from him,
something that is 'extra' to him. The christian calls this inexpressible element God the creator who, precisely because
he is God, throws no shadows over man's existence and can
therefore be present even though he may appear to be absent.
Man's hesitant answer to his own question, which is in the
first place given in praxis, is identified in christian faith.
Man's history, which is God's creation, is thus the condition
for understanding christian revelation and at the same time
the answer given by revelation. The abundance of meaning
which is contained in the meaning man has already discovered in the world is manifested in the light of revelation.
It is therefore not really possible to speak of 'anonymous
christians', even though it is certainly necessary to express in
one way or another the fact that non-christians are not, because of their orthopraxis, deprived of salvation. On the
contrary, christians call themselves such in an explicit, conscious and justified way: with joy because of the identified
mystery which still remains a mystery. In the man Jesus,
man's question about himself and the human answer to this
question are translated into a divine question put to man
and the divine answer to this question: Jesus is the Son of
God, expressed in terms of humanity. He *is* the question-
answer-correlation.

In speaking about God, then, the catholic christian has
become rather less rationalist, without denying the claims
of human intelligibility and justification, and the protestant
christian has become rather less fideist, without denying the
character of revelation as an 'event' or *Ereignis*. This drawing
closer together on both sides can be attributed to the prominence that is given to the hermeneutic question of the human
intelligibility and meaningfulness of christian revelation in
our world. Natural theology is a central theme in contemporary ecumenical discussion because this dialogue between
catholic and protestant is itself essentially orientated towards
the intelligibility of the christian faith for secular man who
is outside the churches. It is obvious that the dialogue is
concentrated not on inter-confessional themes, but on the

questions which man himself asks in his search to transcend himself and contemporary society, in his search for meaning and for a new breathing-space in a world determined by science and technology with their (justified) demands of efficiency and rationality. Ecumenical discussion is directed towards 'questioning man', who is looking for meaning and who is thus able to have a critical function in ecumenical dialogue, so that it will not deteriorate into a fruitless domestic quarrel between two brothers in the same christian family.

6
THE NEW CRITICAL THEORY

I Introductory ideas

A. THE TERM 'CRITICAL THEORY'

The origin of the term 'critical theory' and all that is meant by it is to be found in the critical movement of the enlightenment, which initiated a 'criticism of ideology' in many different spheres. One of the earliest successful ventures was in the field of critical hermeneutics, an attempt by Spinoza to replace the traditional mode of interpretation as practised by orthodox protestants of the period.[62] He developed these new hermeneutics because the bible had become unintelligible to the thinkers of the enlightenment. According to the norms of enlightened reason, 'unintelligible' was the same as 'unreasonable' or 'irrational', with the result that it was impossible, in the opinion of the enlightenment philosophers, to bring the church's tradition, which had become alien to reason, sufficiently up to date by means of hermeneutics for it to be understood. One direct consequence of this was a conflict between the history of interpretation in the church and a more recent tradition, which can be called 'critical', and which includes many aspects of contemporary empirical science, a tradition which has been accompanied by many changes in praxis.

The christian tradition has undoubtedly lost authority as a result of this conflict and in this sense it is possible to say that the hermeneutic reflection initiated by Spinoza contained an element of criticism. This critical intention was lost after the enlightenment, when Schleiermacher in particular dissociated hermeneutics from criticism and practised a new form of 'actualising' interpretation which was very characteristic of the romantic period—continuing and making actual and present the christian interpretation of reality. This tendency was, with certain basic corrections, followed by Dilthey, and has continued since his time, via Heidegger and Gadamer, until now. In this way, hermeneutics has acquired a universal value; as a study, it has become dissociated from the criticism with which it was associated during the enlightenment and its business has become the restoration of the authority of tradition. It has, in one respect, preserved its critical function. It is critical insofar as it has shown the historical consciousness of the period, with its clearly positivist characteristics, to be an objectivist illusion. It has, however, become clear that hermeneutics cannot criticise itself. No one doubts now that tradition is a meaningful whole which is only in need of interpretation because of the different presuppositions that exist between those who initiated the tradition and those who interpret it today.

Since the hermeneutics of the critical kind practised by Spinoza and his successors, and that practised in humane studies (which also contained critical elements, though greatly reduced with the influence of the romantic movement) the marxist interpretation of history and Freudian psychoanalysis have also emerged as critical theory. We may therefore conclude that the term 'critical theory' has become firmly established since the enlightenment.

B. THE 'NEW CRITICAL THEORY'

The critical theory which I shall be discussing in this chapter is rightly known as the 'new critical theory'. The advocates of this theory insist that the critical theory of the enlightenment contained certain speculative and positivist elements. At the same time, however, they aim to pursue consistently the fundamental intention of the enlightenment to its ultimate conclusion, in other words, the realisation of freedom and rationality instead of what has in fact been handed down, an absence of freedom and irrationality. Basically, the enlightenment aimed to contrast this lack of freedom and reason with a critical spirit, which was equally traditional. But the enlightenment must also be seen in the context of the political and even revolutionary movements of emancipation in the

modern era. The thinkers of the enlightenment were aware
of something of which those who practised hermeneutics in
the humane studies had lost sight. Both agreed that we have
to be engaged in dialogue with tradition, in fact that we *are*
dialogue, as Gadamer said, inspired by Heidegger (who is
clearly the best theoretician of hermeneutics as practised in
the sphere of the humanities). The thinkers of the enlightenment, however, recognised that this dialogue with tradition
came up against 'despotic' elements which could even bring
dialogue to an end. In dialogue with tradition a breakdown of
communication can be caused between speaker and listener
or text and reader by a difference in their sphere of understanding; this can be overcome by an 'actualising' interpretation, so that a real understanding is possible. But in the
opinion of the philosophers of the enlightenment there were
also breakdowns in the dialogue with the past which could
not be overcome by hermeneutics. Breakdowns of communication of this kind cannot simply be put right by hermeneutics,
because the suitable answer to them can only be resistance.
For the thinkers of the enlightenment, loss of the authority
of tradition led to the experience of the despotic power of
tradition. Since the claim to authority could not, in accordance with enlightenment thinking, be justified, nor therefore
be freely accepted, it could in fact only assert itself in a despotic manner.

The principle of enlightened reason can therefore be expressed as a demand that all relationships of authority that
are despotic and repressive, in other words, that can only be
justified by the fact that they are there, should be abolished.
In principle, then, the enlightenment was not conscious of any
fundamental opposition between authority and reason. The
philosophers of this period were, however, convinced that
there was, in principle, an opposition between reason as the
principle of non-violent communication and authority in fact,
insofar as it was the agent of a breakdown of communication
of a violent kind, which was a concrete experience in the enlightenment. Looking back at this period in the history of
thought we are now bound to make a distinction between the
critical intention of the thinkers of that period, the basic event
which calls for an actualising continuation, and its many
epiphenomena which were also present, but which do not in
any sense need to be actualised.

It was Horkheimer's aim to renew the critical intention of the enlightenment in the new critical theory, but to divest it of the metaphysical and positivist elements which still clung to it and had not been removed by the enlightenment and the critical movements that resulted from it. This is why the critical theory discussed here is called 'new'. It is essentially anti-metaphysical and is opposed to any philosophy or theology of history which is purely speculative.

C. JURGEN HABERMAS' CRITICAL THEORY OF SOCIETY

This new critical theory has been elaborated in various ways. I shall confine my attention here to the work of the Frankfurt school and to one member of this group especially, Jürgen Habermas. Because of the failure of revolutionary practice, Habermas' predecessors, Adorno, Horkheimer and Marcuse, dissociated their critical theory from praxis and came to regard that theory as, in practice, an impotent protest against society as a system of alienation and objectivisation. According to this view, critical theory is no more than a spark, the memory of which must be kept alive for the coming of the 'completely different', but that this will come about we can in fact only hope and, although this hope is acquired by understanding, it is always associated with doubt.[63] On the other hand, then, this critical theory as expounded by Habermas' predecessors at least in part does not satisfy the demands of science. On the other hand, it is not associated with effective political praxis. For this reason, Habermas has called it a 'new ideology'.

Habermas has recognised that every critical theory runs the risk of becoming dissociated from praxis and thus of losing its critical power. He has therefore given a position of central importance in his own critical theory to the relationship between 'theoretical reason' and 'practical reason'. In his view, critical theory has become dissociated from its original intention, that of being the self-consciousness of a political struggle to emancipate mankind from the despotic relationships which have developed in the course of man's history, both in the communist and in the capitalist countries, to the extent that it was ever present there. Habermas himself has been sharply criticised by the New Left and accused of inconsistency,[64] but there can be no doubt that, inspired by Marx, he has aimed to combine a real critical theory with genuine critical praxis, although he makes a clear distinction between science and political agitation.

Habermas has concluded from the failure of the European revolutionary movements that critical theory has above all to be critical with regard to itself if it is to regain the missing link with political praxis. He has therefore completely disposed of the tendency in contemporary scientific theory to declare itself in principle free of all alien influences and thus 'value-free'. I shall show later in this chapter how radically he criticises this theory of science. In the meantime, it is important to draw attention to a twofold aim in Habermas' activity. In the first place he champions the critical spirit of science and in the second he fights for the scientific spirit of criticism.[65] This is why he has found the spirit of the enlightenment reflected more purely in anti-metaphysical and empirical Anglo-Saxon 'science' than in the 'German thought' of the philosophers of history. In this Anglo-Saxon concept of science, Habermas recognises an element of humanity and progressiveness which is of decisive importance in his own thinking. This element of humanity can be described as anti-metaphysical and self-critical sensibility.

D.   CONDITIONS FOR UNDERSTANDING CRITICAL THEORY

It is necessary to examine three aspects of Habermas' thought more closely if we are to understand his critical theory of history.

1   The emancipative concern of reflection

Habermas has radically criticised the claim that science is value-free. In the name of that claim the empirical sciences and the technology that results from them in fact dictate another system of values to society, which is simply their own—the privileged status of technological rationality.[66] The result of this is that the most difficult human decisions are entrusted to the computer.

On the basis of his analysis, Habermas has concluded that every science is determined by a particular concern. There are basically three of these.

(i) The concern of the analytical and empirical sciences is that of technical usability.[67] In other words, the aim of these sciences is to make prognoses on the basis of the principle of repeatability and in this way to control nature in the service of man. It might also be postulated that the interest of these analytical and empirical sciences is instrumental praxis, which is therefore the condition of these sciences. In this sense, 'reality' is what can be experienced as something that can be used technically.

(ii) The concern of the humane or the hermeneutical sciences is that of communicative praxis.[68] Rules of grammar determine the basis on which intersubjectivity between socialised individuals is achieved or broken down. For these sciences, 'reality' is what lies within the context of people or groups communicating on the basis of a common language. 'The real' is what can be experienced through the interpretation of a valid system of symbols, in other words, a language.

(iii) The concern of the social sciences, which contain elements both of the empirical and analytical sciences and of the hermeneutic sciences, is that of critical or emancipative praxis. This option has enabled Habermas to react against a type of sociology which is orientated exclusively towards a model based either on the natural sciences or on hermeneutics. In his opinion, the scientific concern which ought to determine sociology is above all an explanatory understanding accompanied by a critical theory of society with a practical and historical orientation. The social and technical usability of the social sciences is simply a by-product, but their real concern is an emancipative praxis.[69] To the best of my knowledge, Habermas has not defined what he means by 'reality' in his sociological model but, in my opinion, this could be formulated, in accordance with Habermas' thought, as a view of society under the transcendental condition of what is possible and rational. This definition will be explained in greater detail in the course of this chapter.

This distinction that Habermas has made between communicative, instrumental and critical praxis as the three spheres of concern determining humane studies, the analytical and empirical sciences and the social sciences respectively, defines the objectivity of each of these three branches of science. The three different spheres thus provide the transcendental conditions governing the objectivity that is characteristic of each science.[70] Habermas' analysis of this distinction

is ultimately based on his reflection about contemporary
theory of science and on his deep awareness of the need for
method. At an even deeper level, however, it is inspired by
his new vision of the relationship between theory and praxis,
which is partly marxist in origin, and by his conviction of the
real meaning of reflection. There is an inner bond between
theory and praxis, in which praxis determines theory, in all
three types of science. The determining interests in all scientific knowledge are connected, on the one hand, with their
function in certain settings in life and, on the other, with the
fact that they express a specific inter-relationship between
theory and praxis by which a certain form of social life is
characterised. In Habermas' opinion, praxis determines the
conditions by which man may come to knowledge yet is also
dependent on those processes. This insight has led Habermas
to his functional conviction concerning the real meaning of
reflection. It has also led him to recognise the importance of
the need to analyse the dimension of self-reflection both in
the analytical and empirical sciences and in the humane or
hermeneutic sciences, since only this can reveal the interests
determining them.

If this is done, both technical and communicative praxis
can be directed towards emancipation. Technical praxis is, of
course, directed towards the control of nature but, in this,
there is also the question of man's emancipation from the
violent structures in nature that have not yet been controlled.
The communicative praxis of the hermeneutic sciences is
based on a certain relationship between people in their history
but, in this, there is also the question of man's emancipation
from the violent structures of society that have been handed
down unreflectingly and are the result of political manipulation.

Habermas believes that both these elements of emancipative
interest are based on an even more fundamental and sub-
stantial emancipative interest. The philosopher who inspired
him to undertake this analysis was Fichte, who was, in Habermas' opinion at least, the first thinker to have perceived the
unity that exists between theoretical and practical reason.
Even pure reason is determined by practical reason and the
self-reflection of pure reason is orientated towards praxis, its
practical concern being essentially emancipative and therefore critical. Theory and reflection, Habermas insists, are

directed towards man's emancipation, and both have an emancipative power. On the assumption that human society has come of age, Habermas has stated that 'knowledge and concern are one by virtue of self-reflection'.[71] The emancipative character is essential to the human consciousness and reason is a will to reason, an orientation towards emancipation. Any use of reason, even though it may be called purely theoretical, is bent towards concern, and concern is therefore not alien to reason unless there is an ideological claim for pure reason. Concern belongs to theory as well as to praxis; it precedes knowledge and is realised in knowledge.

This identification of reflective knowledge and emancipative concern underlies not only Habermas' critical theory, but also psychoanalysis, the criticism of ideology and even the philosophy of the enlightenment. This theme of emancipative concern which is the basis of the enlightenment has, according to Habermas, a universal validity and is identical with what is presupposed in all knowledge, in other words, with the concern that is orientated towards being a subject, towards coming of age and towards freedom.

The emancipative and critical power of reflection is therefore at a deeper level than the limited emancipative concern[72] of the humane sciences and the analytical and empirical sciences. This emancipative and critical power therefore cannot be made to depend on instrumental and communicative praxis. If this is done, then science will inevitably reinforce capitalist society and hermeneutics will become an ideology at the service of the dogmatic orthodoxy of the establishment. Unlike other critics, Habermas affirms that the universally valid value of human relationships is an *a priori* presupposition and thus accords a place in the process of communication and hermeneutics to the criticism of ideology.

2   *The psychoanalytical model*

Habermas used the psychoanalytical method as a model for his critical theory of history and for his view of the social sciences. Two aspects have to be distinguished in this special model. First it is a combination of the explanatory type of scientific method (in other words, an exposure of quasi-causal structures) and of the 'understanding' or hermeneutic type, and secondly this theoretical aspect forms a constitutive element of a well defined praxis.

From the practical point of view, the unconscious motives analysed by Freud, which have an influence unknown to the subject who is acting, have the status or function of causes. This is why the behaviour that is analysed can be defined without reference to the underlying motives. The relationships are perceived only by the psychoanalyst. As soon as the patient recognises the interpretation that is formulated by the psychoanalyst as correct, the unconscious motives can be cleared out of the way. Unconscious motives are, so to speak, disguised as causes and they have the power of motives in that disguise and as such.[73]

The recognition of patterns of behaviour which can be interpreted as 'causal' is therefore the point of departure from which social and historical relationships with an objective orientation, as distinct from subjective intentions, can be reconstructed. A knowledge of these connections can break the spell of compulsory actions which are the result of violent structures that are either natural or imposed by tradition. Psychoanalysis, which tries to interpret processes of socialisation with the aid of a universal scheme of interpretation, is therefore an explanatory theory with the practical aim of making pathological processes intelligible and, on the basis of this understanding, curable. The process takes place as explanation, understanding and curative process. In other words, it is an understanding through explanation with a therapeutic praxis in mind. This, then, is a model of interpretation which is not simply interpretative, but which also forms a constitutive part of a praxis.

This psychoanalytical model cannot, of course, have a universal application.[74] It can, however, draw our attention to the fact that a knowledge of quasi-causal laws can enable us to reconstruct certain relationships. This is all the more pertinent because these relationships exist unknown to those concerned and therefore have an influence which is repressive and violent and which can only be broken, both in theory and in practice, if this situation is perceived hermeneutically.

It is clear, then, that the analytical and empirical method is combined in psychoanalysis with the method of the hermeneutic sciences. What is more, Habermas' view of the relationship between theory and praxis is obviously different from that of his predecessors and it forms the basis of his critical theory of society, since something analogous to what has been described above certainly takes place in the social structures within which we live. Finally, three aspects of Habermas' critical theory should be borne in mind in considering what follows. First, there is the hermeneutic understanding of social relationships by, secondly, an explanation of elements of repression and coercion in society which may not, at first sight, be obvious. This scientific understanding by explanation is explicitly framed in order, thirdly, to free society from those elements of compulsion by means of emancipative and if necessary revolutionary practice and, in this way, to initiate a really human history. We may say of this history that it is for the first time really human and that mankind as a social whole can really call itself the free subject of this history. In brief, we can sum up by saying that Habermas aims at understanding by analysis with an emancipative liberation in mind. These three elements are indissolubly connected. If they are separated, the theory becomes uncritical.

3 The continuation of Marx's criticism of society
The members of the Frankfurt school and especially Habermas have, on the one hand, forcefully criticised marxism and, on the other, tried to accept Marx and to find a way of making him acceptable today. This has entailed a revision of his criticism of society in the light of a changed historical situation, a period of 'late capitalism', and on the assumption that man and society are finite. This, of course, is closely linked with Marx' criticism of Feuerbach, who believed that it was possible, if man was truly converted, to emancipate history from its immature dependence on christianity and metaphysics. The result of this change of heart would be in itself a 'better history'. Marx, however, was aware of the radical limitations imposed on human freedom by the existing social situation and therefore concentrated his attention on preparing a detailed analysis of the actual social and economic structures.[75]

The conclusion that the protagonists of the critical theory have drawn from the obvious degeneration of marxist praxis since Stalinism is that marxist theory contains the seeds of a decline of praxis or at least a theoretical correlation of that decline. I cannot go into this thesis here, but must be content to point briefly to the nature of the speculative element in marxist thought as outlined by these contemporary thinkers.[76]

In the first place, they maintain, it was based on a residual
metaphysical philosophy stemming from Hegel and interpreted as a transition to revolution. Secondly, it consisted of an
eschatological tendency to make the proletariat absolute on
the one hand and, on the other, a tendency to raise the concept of work to the status of an ideology both in the marxist
theory of history and in the idea of revolution. Despite the
fact that they have criticised Marx's philosophy in this way,
however, they have taken it over as the basis of their new
critical theory, because they are convinced that Marx has
presented the critical, emancipative spirit of the enlightenment in its most authentic form.

II An outline of the new 'critical theory of society'

Since the new critical theory is above all a serious attempt to
understand modern society by explanation in the light of an
emancipative interest, I shall refer to it either as a 'critical
theory of history' or as a 'critical theory of society'. Basing my
arguments on the books and articles listed in this chapter, I
shall also try to conceptualise this critical theory point by
point. It is necessary, however, to say at the outset that this
exposition will inevitably include an element of abstraction,
because it is principally an attempt to outline in a convenient
and easily surveyed form what can be found scattered throughout all the writings of Habermas and the other protagonists
of critical theory.

A.   A RATIONAL AND EMPIRICALLY DEDUCED THEORY

In the first place, the critical theory of history is critical of
the traditional philosophy of history with its idealistic flavour.
The new social order which the protagonists of this theory
aim to achieve is not in any sense the realisation of an ideal
and cannot be theoretically anticipated. It is, on the contrary,
the result of a reaction to the experience of an absence of
freedom in society and it can therefore only come about
by means of praxis. Critical theory is not based on a positive
image of man or society. It is rather based on the insight that
has developed only in the modern era, namely that mankind is capable of making history in a free and rational way.
(This will be discussed in greater detail later in section B.)
Theory and praxis are not, however, based on a philosophical
insight into man's being.

The critical theory of society, then, does not analyse social relationships by means of a norm based on one particular image of man; all that it does is to investigate the factual structure and the articulation of those relationships. This analysis must be carried out again and again. The obvious conclusion from this is that we cannot continue to apply Marx' analysis of the social and economic situation of his own times to society in the second half of the twentieth century.

This theory therefore analyses the idea that men have formed of the good life, in other words, it examines the image of man that they in fact have and use. This can be discovered from an analysis of social relationships and what emerges from this is that there has always been, either consciously or unconsciously, a positive image of man and society underlying the organisation or articulation of society in every period of history and underlying all that society's institutions. An understanding of that image of man and society leads to a revelation of the limitations and the lack of freedom in specific social groupings and institutions. This exposure of the image of man which is, at least initially, usually unconscious and which underlies the articulations of the most important social relationships is a necessary condition for the eventual overcoming of the limitations and the lack of freedom that characterise the establishment.

C. B. McPherson, for example, has revealed by analysis[77] that the implicit image of man underlying European and North American societies is basically democratically liberal and individualistic. In a similar way, critical theory attempts to expose the functional and disfunctional relationships that exist in the development of means of production on the one hand and, on the other, the forms of power that are assumed. In its analysis of society, then, critical theory discovers repressive and despotic structures which had not been noticed before, at least directly, in social relationships. Because of its interest in the emancipative history of freedom, it concentrates sociologically on precisely these elements of compulsion. What is more, because of this orientation, and because it freely makes use of sociological methods, critical theory is sometimes known as 'critical sociology'. Just as the psychoanalyst discovers unconscious motives which, disguised in unconscious causes, have a repressive influence on the patient's behaviour, so too does the critical theoretician discover, by analysing the factual social system, all kinds of quasi-causal relationships which, in a hidden way, make their influence felt on human behaviour. The disclosure of these quasi-causal relationships in society is a first step towards man's emancipation.

B.   CRITICAL THEORY AS THE SELF-CONSCIOUSNESS OF A PRAXIS

Critical theory aims at a theoretical understanding which essentially accompanies an emancipative praxis. The analysis of social relationships does not aim to collect a theoretical knowledge of 'what is'—scientific knowledge of this is irreplaceable.[78] Scientific analysis aims to collect knowledge of what can be and of what must be, though this may be negative, as will appear later. This analysis does in fact also produce knowledge of what is, but the aim of the analysis is above all an emancipative praxis. It explains its knowledge of what is in the formal sense of what can be and not, for example, in the sense of what must necessarily be or of what ought ethically to be or even of what is eternally valid.

In critical theory, then, the reconstruction of history is at the service of its interest in a reconstruction of contemporary social relationships and this interest functions precisely as a criticism of those relationships. In other words, the understanding that critical theory has in mind is a historical understanding of repressive relationships insofar as they are experienced as violent, and of the justification of coercion and domination insofar as this is experienced as untrue. The aim of this understanding is to clear these relationships out of the way.[79] It is clear, then, that what is involved here is a model of interpretation which can be used to enable society to understand itself, above all in the sense of the alienations that are present in that society. The special characteristic of this model, however, is that it is not simply a model of interpretation. On the contrary, the interpretation is inwardly linked to a critical praxis of contestation of these social structures. The interest in knowledge is identical with the interest in emancipative praxis, which is an enlightened praxis determined by scientifically explanatory interpretation.

At the basis of critical theory there is a certain working hypothesis or presupposition, namely that, since mankind has become one social whole, we are able, as free, responsible human beings, to make history ourselves. In other words, at the level of reason and freedom, we can control the structures which determine our being. This hypothesis is not imposed as a necessity on the analysis of society, nor is the point of departure for this analysis a particular religious, ethical or humanist image of man which might in turn impose on us the task of making our history freely and responsibly ourselves. The point of departure is an empirically deduced theory. This means that, since the beginning of the modern era, and even more in recent years, mankind has become more and more a social whole which can itself become the subject of history.[80] It is only now that mankind has reached the point where it can really direct its history towards one clearly defined aim. According to Habermas, the validity of any philosophy of history depends on two basic presuppositions—that history is one and that it can be made by free, rational men. A rationalisation of any philosophy of history is therefore only possible if history is effectively brought about by free, rational men. This has been the case since the seventeenth and eighteenth centuries and it has only become quite clear in the nineteenth and twentieth centuries.

The immanent presuppositions of a history of philosophy have only been realised in our own times, the period in which the power to rationalise history has developed. It was only when the capitalist system of production had become firmly established that the earlier feudal structures were completely replaced in an increasing number of social relationships by the system of exchange and that more and more institutions in society at the same time ceased to be regarded as natural events. The decline of the feudal pattern of production and the rise of bourgeois society with its emphasis on the autonomy of the individual were also accompanied by a process of rationalisation in many spheres. The idea that it was possible for man to make history himself took root at this time, together with a growing conviction, stemming from the enlightenment, that history could be rationally controlled. The question of a philosophy of history therefore arose as the result of objective tendencies in history in a chronologically datable phase of its development. As a consequence of the industrialisation of society and its technically perfected social intercourse in the twentieth century, the mutual interdependence of political events and the integration of social relationships have advanced to the point where, within this contemporary structure of communications, 'history has become united as a history of the *one* world'.[81]

It is therefore evident that it was not until quite late that history became one and that man became able to make it himself—these two aspects of history did not even exist as a possibility before a certain period—and, as a consequence, it would be wrong to project these two characteristics back into the 'history' preceding the modern era. Habermas' conclusion is that it is an unjustified ideology to postulate a total meaning for the whole of history either in philosophy or in theology. In the past, history was simply not determined by one subject. It is only in the modern era that it has become possible to deduce on the basis of empirical data that history can be made by free, rational men. This means, Habermas insists, that there can be no abstract and theoretical speculative statement which is valid for all periods in history. It is only in the present period of history that the natural and coercive elements of the past could be replaced by communication between all men, theoretically at the rational level and practically at the level of true democratic order. At the rational level and at the level of freedom, it has become possible to expose and to control quasi-causal social relationships. Theoretical analysis has made this possibility empirically clear. It is not possible to deduce it speculatively nor can it be imposed by religious, ethical or humanist views of man and the world. One consequence of Habermas' thesis is that it is not possible for man to speculate idealistically about the total meaning of history, but that it has, since the advent of the modern era, become possible to give a meaning and indeed a total one to a history that can be made freely by men.

C.   CRITICAL THEORY AS A THEORY OF WHAT IS ACTUALLY
      POSSIBLE

Critical theory has shown, empirically and scientifically rather than on the basis of a rationally unjustifiable option, that it is theoretically and practically not impossible to oppose the idea that history is determined by powers such as the establishment, or chance or unconscious motives or a particular image of man.[82] The historically developed social structures are apparently in fact such as to exclude the possibility.[83] Critical theory has revealed that what seems to be inevitable is in fact contingent and therefore changeable. The practical impossibility of breaking through the present order is the result of existing structures which are contingent. By changing these structures, what is 'possible and rational' but was in practice impossible can be made feasible. The discovery made by analysis that the coercive elements present in the world are historically contingent has brought to light what is possible and rational. In this way, critical theory has been able to show that a breach exists between the contemporary structures of social relationship (which should not be regarded as necessary or as historically determined, at the risk of propagating an ideology) and the possibilities of those structures. The consequence of this is that reason and freedom are certainly possible in our own time. Critical analysis has revealed that, quite apart from religious, humane and ethical imperatives, a different articulation of the various scientific and real practices is possible and, what is more, that this possibility is to everyone's advantage. Only a practical transformation of the whole social structure can in fact make what is objectively possible cease to be in fact impossible and what is objectively irrational cease to be in fact necessary.

It would seem, then, that emancipative or critical praxis is the only way in which what is possible and rational can be realised. Praxis has therefore to be regarded as taking precedence over any theory on which a religious, ethical or philosophical image of man is based. The *necessity* of a revolutionary change in actual social relationships, with their coercive elements which are determined by capitalism or by socialist-inspired state capitalism, is therefore in fact dependent on the *possibility* of that revolution. What is possible is, by its very nature, something that necessarily has to be realised, since the fundamental interest towards which critical theory is directed is the emancipative history of freedom. In other words, according to critical theory, anything presented to us as possible freedom has to be realised.

Marcuse's formulation of this idea is more utopian: he maintains that revolution is possible because it is necessary. The later protagonists of critical theory, on the other hand, claim that it is necessary because it is clear from critical analysis that it is possible, and because the basic presupposition of that analysis is man's will to emancipation. The critical theory of society can in this sense be called an optimism of human reason because and insofar as it expresses a practical possibility by which what is possible and rational can *de facto* become the determining factor in man's history. Only a scientific analysis of the concrete social configuration can throw light on the possible conditions of a revolution and provide a critical basis for its practical necessity. As Habermas has commented, 'to that extent, revolutionary theory is the doctrine of categories of criticism'.[84]

It should be noted in this context that the determining factor here is the scientific analysis which leads to understanding. There can be no place in critical theory for an interpretation of what society ought to be in the light of a theoretical ideal. Clearly, then, a change has taken place here in the relationship between theory and praxis. What has been suggested is a scientific theory of history or of society which is first based on an analytical knowledge of factual social relationships and which secondly effectively results in a revolution which realises a completely different society. Just as, in psychoanalysis, there is a therapeutic result when the patient accepts fully the psychiatrist's treatment and 'understands by explanation', so too is there revolutionary praxis when there is acceptance of the theoretical analysis, an 'understanding by explanation' of the existing social relationships. Finally, the emancipative interest determining critical theory can only be aroused by an experience of violence and suffering, in other words, by the experience of a breakdown in communication. This question will be discussed in the following section.

D. THE HYPOTHETICAL CHARACTER AND CRITICAL NEGATIVITY
   OF CRITICAL THEORY

The diagnosis which critical theory has made of society and its plan for future praxis can only be realised in its actual result, in other words, when all those who have experienced a change brought about by this theory freely recognise this as a real emancipation.[85] As such, critical theory is clearly simply hypothetical: it can only be understood as an element of factual, experimental praxis, with the result that the criterion of its success is successful emancipation itself. In the same way, even an anticipation of the end of history is also purely hypothetical.[86] This cannot be regarded as a kind of pragmatism, according to which it might be postulated that critical theory is true because it is successful. On the contrary, the very reverse is more correct: because the critical theory is true, it is successful. The only criterion for the validity of critical theory is the scientific reliability of its sociological analyses as borne out by an emancipative praxis. Put in a different way, we may say that its criterion is critical rationality, at least insofar as this is linked to a critical praxis.[87]

But so long as this theory is not realised, its necessity and its validity are no more than hypothetical. It is true that it anticipates a restructuring of the whole of society in its affirmation that this new structure does not yet exist, but that it is possible. This anticipation, however, is not based on a theoretical value or on an ideal, nor is it a conclusion drawn from a philosophy of history: on the contrary, it is purely critical and negative. Critical theory, in other words, has to restrict itself to making negative statements about a better society in the future; it cannot say anything positive about that future society and therefore should not aim to. The anticipation of the future society is itself no more than critical speech about contemporary society and effective opposition to it. It is precisely for this reason that the critical theory of history or of society is characterised by the findings of empirical analysis and also why it is at the same time critical, in contrast to a theology or a philosophy of history. It can therefore provide us with an explanatory analysis of contemporary society, but it cannot describe what will or must be effective in the future. It stands between these two poles as pure criticism of the contemporary establishment and, since it rejects as a point of departure a religious, ethical or philosophical ideal concerning the future, it can, even now, perform only a critically negative function.

Critical theory does not deny the importance of the question asked by the philosophy of history,[88] but it dissociates itself from any purely theoretical answer to that question, from any ideology of evolutionary progress and from any appeal to a predictable course in history, either in the materialist or in the spiritualist sense. It even dissociates itself from E. Bloch's 'ontology of the not yet', which has been suggested as a substitute for revolutionary practice.[89] Critical theory also dismisses any positive philosophy which attempts to define man's 'being' and thus envisages something other than his actual historical existence. It also rejects the classical marxist standpoint that the proletariat is the special class in society which is or will be responsible for the definition of the total meaning of history as an eschatological sacralisation of the working class, a raising of it to the level of a fetish. Critical theory is, in other words, limited to an empirically deduced theory which is opposed to all ideology.[90]

It should be clear from this why a fundamental aspect of critical theory is that an appeal can never be made, in an attempt to justify or guarantee criticism,[91] to elements that are alien to scientific analysis or to the possibilities of emancipative praxis. Criticism cannot have an ideological substructure. If it is not to lose its validity, it must always be critically negative. It can only be justified by contemporary theoretical and practical possibilities. In this respect, it cannot be said that it is nihilistic or anarchistic, even though it has to be admitted that it can only function now by contestation and contradiction. The ultimate basis of this contestation of contemporary structures, however, is that these are so rigid that they prevent other possibilities from being realised and, at least in principle, critical theory limits itself to these inhibiting aspects of contemporary structures. Critical theory, then, is consistent only insofar as it opposes not what has been accomplished, but the inclination that is shown by what is already achieved to perpetuate itself and to hinder the realisation of possibilities.

This 'understanding by analytical explanation' of contemporary social structures, with its essential aspect of criticism of actual society, is the only justification of critical theory. Consequently some scholars have said that criticism is bound to disappear as soon as the present social situation has *de facto* been changed.

E. CRITICAL THEORY AS A MEDIATION BETWEEN THEORY AND PRAXIS

The critical theory of history aims to be a rational mediation between emancipative praxis and the appropriation of reality by knowledge. If this central position of critical theory between theory and praxis and the consequent reconciliation of theory and praxis are ignored, critical theory is at once deprived of its fundamental intention of being a 'theoretical practice' and transformed into an ideology at the service of a group of critics in a party or in the establishment. If this happens, 'understanding by explanation' at once becomes the privilege of a special élite and this is obviously counter to the

principle that emancipative freedom is sought for the sake of
all men. The result of this private intellectual possession on
the part of individuals or of a special group is that only the
class of people who are already in possession will gain any
advantage. Emancipation is not, however, something that is
carried out by the theoreticians of history. On the contrary,
it is achieved by those who effectively change the contemporary articulation of social relationships. Existing society will
naturally try to integrate its critics tolerantly and in this way
to neutralise them, taking care that the social order remains
unchanged. This has in fact happened many times, the
critics of society being called 'revisionists'. The existing social
order is always ready to acknowledge that its critics have a
full right to exist, on condition that they confine their criticism
to an attempt to adapt society in a limited way, so that it remains basically the same. This, of course, means that the
critics are in fact bound to deny their fundamental intention.
As a result of this situation, many critics believe that they
have to stand outside the existing system if they are effectively
to criticise it; if they remain within it, they will, they think,
become once again encapsulated.

The advantage gained by the establishment if the critics of
society stand outside the system is, of course, that it is rid of
its annoying opponents and no longer has to put up with the
irritation of those who reveal the existing order as a system in
which freedom and reason are absent. If the critics are outside the system, they can easily be made the objects of suspicion and branded as a group that is hostile to society.
Criticism may, in this sense, degenerate to the level of anarchy,
but what is more likely to happen is that those who are true
to the establishment often view the departure of those who
attack the social system with gladness, while those critics who
do not depart are neutralised and integrated, with the result
that everything remains the same.

Those who aim to be completely consistent in their critical
theory therefore insist that it must be indissolubly linked with
revolutionary praxis. On the other hand, Habermas has shown
in the 'seminar/theses' that he wrote in reaction to an action
group of students of philosophy and sociology at Frankfurt
University[92] that preparation for political action should not in
any sense form a 'part of seminar activity'. Although he regards praxis as an essential part of scientific activity, he is

opposed to any 'scientific taking by storm'. As he himself has said, 'The consequence of the systematic unity of theory and praxis is not a unity of scientific analysis and immediate preparation for political action. This is why the appeal to the unity of theory and praxis cannot justify a demand for an institutional unity of science and preparation for action. It is necessary to separate the two spheres'. A little later, he states that there are 'structural differences between science and preparation for action which call for a clear institutional separation of the two spheres. If one is confused with the other, both are bound to be damaged. Science is corrupted under the pressure of action and political action is inevitably led astray by a pseudo-scientific alibi'.

Habermas is thus clearly opposed both to left-wing activism and to the reactions to it—the very reactions which provide the activists with a welcome excuse for action. For Habermas, both the scientific character of critical theory and the critical character of scientific analysis are sacred and this is above all why he cannot accept a merging together of scientific analysis and political action. This is clear evidence of Habermas' resolute adherence to what he regards as the fundamental idea of the enlightenment: 'The basis of the enlightenment is that science is tied to the principle that discussion must be free of power structures and that it is tied to no other principle'. He is firmly convinced that any attack against this fundamental principle of the enlightenment makes enlightened political action impossible. If thought and science are made instruments of the needs of the moment in so-called praxis, the very conditions of enlightened reason are undermined and, with them, the very foundations of humanity.[93]

F.   THE IMPOSSIBILITY OF FORMALISING CRITICAL THEORY

It has often been affirmed that, as a form of self-criticism, critical theory cannot be formalised. As soon as any attempt is made to do this, it becomes ambivalent. It is, after all, a criticism directed towards the contemporary articulation of social relationships and not towards social structures as such. Consistent with its point of departure, critical theory therefore states that what it presents as its content can only be the result of the analysis of a concrete historical configuration, in other words, that of a given society at a given period, of which it exposes the anatomy, so to speak. The theory cannot be abstracted from the actual situation and this means that it is bound to depend on new analyses whenever social structures change. This is why it has correctly been called a science without 'orthodoxy'. The factual reality towards which it is directed is not measured against consistent ethical, religious or philosophical values, nor is it measured against any utopian value. It is simply analysed with a dissecting knife so that criticism can be directed towards it. In view of this, it would be wrong to give this theory of contradiction as such a transcendental philosophical significance. Some successors and imitators of the critical theory succeed, it is true, in giving the impression that they have discovered the true transcendental philosophy in it and even a transcendental understanding of all religious feeling, but the most convincing protagonists of the theory reject this idea.

I shall, in the following chapter, confront this critical theory with theological hermeneutics and try to evaluate the important perspectives that this confrontation opens up.

7
THE NEW CRITICAL THEORY AND THEOLOGICAL HERMENEUTICS

In the previous chapter I considered whether the 'new critical theory', as evolved by the Frankfurt school and especially by Jürgen Habermas, might perhaps lead to an extension of theological hermeneutics. The outline that I provided in that chapter of the concepts and the basic principles of the critical theory of society and history should form the basis of a direct confrontation between that critical theory and theological hermeneutics. Before bringing this confrontation about, however, I think it is worthwhile to consider briefly some general philosophical aspects of the question. There will be ample opportunity to situate the specific critical observations that are made in this section in the subsequent, more strictly theological reflection.

I Preliminary critical remarks
A. THE IMPLICIT HERMENEUTIC CIRCLE OF CRITICAL THEORY

In an interview on German television, I recently heard the old philosopher Martin Heidegger say that Marx, in the first part of his well-known statement, 'philosophers interpret the world, but the point is to change it', denies what is implicitly presupposed in the second half. Certainly, to assert that the world has to be changed implies a certain interpretation of reality and is itself already an interpretation. I found myself thinking about this quotation from Marx in studying the critical theory of society, which again and again claims to be based exclusively on scientific analysis and to depend in no way on religious or ethical values. Yet an appeal to the movement of emancipative freedom is essential to these analyses. Assuming that all other ideological values are suspect, why should not emancipation and freedom also be the ideals of a repressive and despotic society? In other words, the critical theory is not based exclusively on scientific analysis. It depends in the first place on a fundamental ethical option in favour of emancipation and freedom.[94] I personally can only applaud this choice. The decision to oppose all kinds of manipulation and to defend human freedom is an ethical action of the first importance and is quite independent of the question of what we are to do with this freedom in the world once it has been divested of all compulsion. However acceptable it may be, this choice is nonetheless an ethical decision, an existential option. It does not as such follow from the contingency of scientifically analysed structures, but presupposes an interpretation of our humanity, even if this is simply a very specific kind of hermeneutics. Despite the assertions of those who have evolved it, then, critical theory takes place within the so-called hermeneutic circle, because it implies a philosophy of man and this in turn presupposes an implicit interpretation of our humanity. This is why critical theory cannot be used as a meta-theory in relation to philosophical and theological hermeneutics—its scientifically conditioned interpretation of reality proceeds from a hermeneutics which is accepted as meaningful.

Some of the protagonists of the critical theory of society, such as Wellmer,[95] believe that the idea of a history of emancipative freedom becomes a 'problematical prejudice' as soon as it is used as a slogan for emancipative criticism.[96] Criticism on the basis of scientific analysis, Wellmer insists, can only become a living reality within the framework of a successful emancipative revolutionary praxis, because the only way in which we can confirm—that is, verify or falsify—the anticipation of possible freedom as expressed negatively by critical theory is in a new state of experienced freedom. It is also only in this way that universal consent will be given to it. In this, however, Wellmer maintains, a praxis based on emancipative criticism will continue to degenerate if it is based on a 'structural danger to emancipative praxis, as long as this praxis is only able to take place in conditions of broken communications', in other words, in modern conditions. The protagonists of the new critical theory will have therefore to accept the fact that they are still in the dark with regard to the future of the praxis of this theory and that this future cannot, by definition, be known, with the consequence that they have to base their conclusions on a theoretical working hypothesis. This is, however, based in turn on a personal option in favour of the history of emancipative freedom, which was the fundamental thrust of the enlightenment and, as we pointed out in the previous chapter, one of the foundations of true humanity. As a result of this situation, we are bound to conclude that we have the idea of 'freedom' at our disposal as men who are not yet free, which is as much as to say that we do not have it at our disposal at all. Freedom is for us a utopian idea which thrusts human history forward on its course, gradually compelling it to yield certain results.

This freedom is also a situated freedom. It is possible for us to ask whether critical theory does not make use of a fictitious concept of absolute freedom which is essentially opposed to human possibilities. From the critical point of view, the historical question of what must be preserved is as justified as the emancipative question of what should be changed. Ultimately, the demand for freedom cannot be satisfied by freedom without content, although we are bound to admit that freedom from manipulation is of enormous value. The aims of the critical theory cannot be refuted simply by appealing to our human situation, because this can also degenerate into an ideology. The limitations imposed on all that man can do are certainly real, but these possibilities are part of the historical process and, within the limits of man's corporeality and his being a person in a social system, it is impossible to establish *a priori* or theoretically the actual possibilities or impossibilities of man's being. It is therefore often useless to ask whether it is, in view of our human situation, possible to achieve something: the question is often the result of a failure to appreciate the pressure exercised by utopian ideals on the reality of our humanity, although this may be very limited. It nonetheless remains true to say that humanity is fundamentally a possibility of freedom. Freedom has to be fought for again and again in the contemporary situation on the basis of man's physical nature, which situates it in history, in structures and in situations which both support freedom and threaten to alienate it from itself. In changing historical forms,

this is part of the essence of our historically situated humanity. It is a threat which can never be fully eliminated. On the
basis of humane and christian motives, however, the believer
—and especially the theologian—must play a critical but
active part in the history of emancipative freedom. In any
case, it is an ethical and prophetic task for the christian community to find out, by means of critical analysis, what repressive and violent elements are concealed in society. This task
forms an essential part of the contemporary need to make the
christian message present, active and credible in the world
today and to prevent it from degenerating into an ideology.

B.   OBJECTIONS TO RADICAL CRITICAL NEGATIVITY

We must now consider the radical critical negativity connected
with critical theory. It should be clear from certain comments in my writings that I attach a great deal of importance
to negative dialectics in general and that I have given particular attention to this concept in the work of the Frankfurt
school. It has, however, always been my aim to stress the fact
that these negative dialectics are sustained by a positive sphere
of meaning which will direct praxis, even though this can
only be expressed in a pluralist way. In critical theory, however, there is no absolute value and there is also considerable
resistance to what is known in the theory as the process of
making certain values into a fetish or putting them under
absolute taboo. (It will, of course, have been clear from the
preceding comment that the value of 'emancipative freedom'
is not included among these fetishes.)

There is, of course, a tendency to make negativity itself into
a new fetish and to intensify 'no' until it becomes an absolute,
and this in turn favours the growth of a new form of alienation. According to critical theory, the concept of critical negativity has developed from the scientific analysis of actual social
structures, and this analysis is therefore the source from which
what is possible and real is rationally deduced. In fact, however, the concept is either a negative absolutism, or else it
implies a positive sphere of meaning, but that would give a
relative value to the radical nature of critical negativity. On
the basis of my conclusions about the importance and meaning of experiences of contrast and of negative dialectics,[97] I
am unable to accept a *philosophie du non*[98] if this is not sup-
ported and made relative by an option, which is in fact an

ethical and philosophical choice made for the purpose of achieving meaning in history. In other words, this 'no' also presupposes a hermeneutical process which is based on meaning and not on nonsense. We therefore come down to what we have already said in the comment made in the preceding section, namely that the negative dialectics of critical theory are only meaningful insofar as they really presuppose and imply the possibility of a hermeneutics which make meaning present and actual, whether this is the intention or not.

C. THE ANALYSIS OF NONSENSE

It should be clear from what I have said in the preceding section that my objections to the critical theory of society have been in the main directed against its claim to be purely analytical. In fact, however, it presupposes a hermeneutic process which is not explicitly recognised as such and accepts *a priori* the importance and the meaning of emancipative freedom. It is also remarkable that, by comparison with the hermeneutics which look for meaning in history, critical theory has swung round almost one hundred and eighty degrees and, at least in its analysis, looks only for lack of meaning, which is certainly present in history. The contrast may be expressed in the following way: the hermeneutic tradition looks in history for what can be made present again, while critical theory looks for what cannot be made present again. Both approaches are fully justified, since history is an insane complex of sense and nonsense. Those who practised the hermeneutic sciences or the humanities had to some extent forgotten that our relationship with the past contains elements of division and justified opposition. Now, however, those who practise critical theory seem to forget that thought (one form or another of philosophical, reflective thought) has an original relationship with what comes to us through tradition in the form of meaning already acquired. This shortsightedness reminds one of Heidegger's 'forgetfulness of being'.

A first, provisional confrontation between the analytic tendency of critical theory and the hermeneutic tendency of theology (and of philosophy) is therefore already possible. This confrontation is inevitable for two principal reasons. In the first place, theology is essentially a hermeneutic undertaking, because it attempts to make the meaning that has been proclaimed in history present here and now in our contemporary existence, whereas critical theory opens our eyes above all to the elements of nonsense in our existence, those elements for which history is also responsible. The second reason for this confrontation is that modern theology prefers, rightly, to use the behavioural or social sciences as one of its points of departure. The principal question then is whether this point of departure is, in the terminology of critical theory, the sociology of the establishment or a social science which is 'critical'. It has, however, to be recognised that, if theology does not make use of the second (critical) form of sociology, it is always in grave danger of becoming an ideology, both by presenting and continuing the christian message that has been expressed in history and by its appeal to the humanities in this process.

Since the enlightenment theology has, by comparison with the earlier *hermeneutica profana* and *hermeneutica sacra,* become hermeneutic in a completely new way, having been made more sensitive by the loss of traditional authority. Spinoza was one of the first to evolve a form of critical hermeneutics by his deep awareness of the fact that our relationship with the past contains elements of division. In theology, however, the romantic reduction of the concept of understanding quickly gained the upper hand, with the result that critical hermeneutics soon became identified with Schleiermacher's 'new hermeneutics'. Later, Dilthey became the main exponent of this new hermeneutic science. He certainly inherited the critical spirit of the enlightenment, but his main concern was to restore the meaning handed down by tradition to which full justice was no longer done because of the breakdown in modern communications. Closely related to these hermeneutics are the 'new' hermeneutic projects of Rudolf Bultmann and his successors, Gerhard Ebeling and Ernst Fuchs especially.[99] These hermeneutics are based on the one hand on the younger Heidegger and on the other on the older Heidegger and have been formulated in a classical manner by H. G. Gadamer. There is certainly a connection between hermeneutics and criticism in these later 'new' systems of hermeneutics, expressed especially in Heidegger's 'hermeneutic circle'[100] which has been given the better title of 'hermeneutic spiral' by the French historian H. Marrou and the American theologian Ray Hart.[101] After all, a circular movement is unending.

Within the hermeneutic circle, there is an interaction between our understanding of traditional relationships of meaning and the constant correction of our own pre-understanding.
This critical, corrective impulse goes back in practice to the
dominant claim of the tradition that we are aiming to make
present. The apparent point of departure is the presupposition
that what is handed down in tradition, and especially the
christian tradition, is always meaningful, and that this meaning only has to be deciphered hermeneutically and made present and actual. The fact that tradition is not only a source
of truth and unanimity, but also a source of untruth, repression and violence is not forgotten in hermeneutics, but it is
also not considered systematically. At least as a theme, this
particular insight of the enlightenment has found no place in
the hermeneutics of the humane sciences as used by theologians.
With its own special method, this form of hermeneutics can
therefore discover the breakdowns of communication in
the dialogue with history which are the result of original
differences in the sphere of understanding, but not those
which are the result of repressive and violent power structures that already exist as given in any society. With precisely this last category in mind, critical theory presents us
with the possibility of an extension of hermeneutic reflection,
which can be brought about especially by this critical theory
in view of the particular orientation of its model of interpretation. It has in fact discovered a new dimension in the
hermeneutic process of understanding. It not only takes into
account the breakdowns in historical communication between
men from case to case, but also gives a central place in its
investigations to the analysis of the significance and the compelling logic of such breakdowns. It conducts a systematic
analysis of the violent structural elements present in every
social system.

In view of this model of interpretation, it is clear that
critical theory does not aim to make the past present today
so much as to provide a key for a hermeneutic understanding
which is a criticism of tradition to the extent that we cannot
find ourselves in it 'as in a dialogue'. This kind of hermeneutic understanding is not just directed towards pure communication, as the hermeneutics based on the humane sciences
certainly are, but rather towards an emancipation from repression and domination, which are experienced as a failure

and as an alienation and can therefore be criticised as 'historically entirely superfluous'. The hermeneutic process is really an 'understanding of tradition *against* tradition'[102] and is therefore an emancipation from tutelage in subjection to tradition insofar as this is a context of compulsion. This kind of understanding is at the same time also the condition for emancipation at the level of praxis.

This model of interpretation can be accused of one-sidedness, but it is certainly justified. In any case, why should this one-sided interest be any less important than an equally one-sided interest in the meaningful elements of tradition? It is problematic to attempt to make traditional meaning present and actual without having clearly in mind what cannot be made present—and vice versa.

We have already seen in these comments that the right of an actualising theology to exist is not violated by critical theory, because this theory implicitly, none the less really, presupposes that hermeneutics are meaningful. All the same, it is difficult to understand why the implicit hermeneutic circle of critical theory should be justified and why the explicit hermeneutic circles of the hermeneutic sciences are not justified. Critical theory correctly directs the attention of hermeneutical theologians in a systematic way towards aspects which they, in their preoccupation with making tradition present, tend to forget. Critical theory draws their attention to the contingent aspect of tradition which is often apparently hypostatised in theological hermeneutics. In the hermeneutics of the humane sciences, after all, a methodological abstraction is made of this contingent aspect and of the contestive criticism that is evoked by it. As a consequence, theologians, both in their historical investigations and in their 'actualising' reflections, often have a barely concealed idealist concept of history. They tend to regard the history of the church's *kerygma* and her dogmas purely as a kind of history of ideas. This autonomous development of ideas remains enclosed within speculation about faith and perpetuates itself on the basis of purely internal *aporias* which can only be solved by a process of speculative thought and dialogue, which in turn give rise to new speculative *aporias* and so on. The whole of man's history thus takes place within a purely theoretical circle of thought. Reference to the classical manuals of the history of dogma confirms the suspicion that there is at least an element of truth in this judgement. There is no need to assert that those who specialise in the history of dogma have no feeling for the findings of critical theory—most of them have a strong enough sense of reality. On the other hand, however, it cannot be claimed that they have given enough deliberate and systematic attention to those aspects that particularly concern modern man, who consciously wishes to take his place in the history of emancipative freedom. No apostolically orientated theology can afford to ignore this or it will degenerate into an esoteric study which no outsider will understand.

In the light of the salutary challenge presented by critical theory to theology, I should like to state explicitly that hermeneutic theology must be inspired by a practical and critical intention.[103] This implies that the orthopraxis that has been discussed repeatedly in previous chapters of this book is an essential element of the hermeneutical process. Although it is, of course, possible to dispute precisely what may be called *orthos* in our praxis, it is in any case certain, on the basis of both human and christian motivation, that any praxis which manipulates human freedom and brings about alienation is both wrong and heterodox. If this criterion were taken seriously into account, we should make considerable progress!

It is therefore clear that a theologically actualising interpretation is not possible without a critical theory which acts as the self-consciousness of a critical praxis. If the unity of faith takes place in real history, in other words, if it is itself really history, then we must not hope to be able to attain unity in faith either purely hermeneutically or by means of a purely theoretical theological interpretation. History is a flesh and blood affair and what has come about in history— the divisions in the christian church, for instance—can never be put right by purely theoretical means. History is an experience of reality which takes place in a series of conflicts, which can only be resolved if the theory used is really the self-consciousness of a praxis. I would therefore agree with J. B. Metz's contention that the historical identity which christianity has lost cannot be regained by making christian traditions present and actual again purely theoretically.[104] Christianity is, in its very being and therefore also in its history, much more than simply a history of interpretation. A purely theoretical interpretation of christianity, an 'orthodoxy' based on an idealist view of history, will in our own times inevitably come into conflict with the problems with which the reality of history itself confronts us. The churches are really the 'community of God' and the 'temple of the Holy Spirit', with the result that we are bound to speak about this in the language of faith. At the same time, however, the churches are also historical and contingent. 'The earthly church and the church enriched with heavenly things . . . are not to be considered as two realities' (*Lumen gentium* 8).

D. CULTURAL REVOLUTION OR SOCIAL AND ECONOMIC STRUCTURAL CHANGE?

Is it possible to claim that a universal subject—an individual, society, 'mankind'—within history contains the course of its development and directs that development? Anyone who does assert this can nowadays expect to be sharply criticised by philosophers, who have shown that ideology and totalitarianism inevitably result if we take as our point of departure the fact that history is governed by a secular universal subject and that a total meaning, which can be embodied in a system or a programme of action, is contained in the individual, in human society or in history itself. This idea can also be defined by affirming that the individual, society and history do not have their ground and their total meaning in themselves, in other words, that they are contingent. The individual, society and history cannot put themselves forward as absolute; they are not identical with themselves. The christian believer will, of course, interpret this fact in the light of his faith in God's creation and say that the individual, society and history have their ground and their total meaning in the living God, who puts them forward in their autonomy. This faith implies that the believer entrusts himself and the whole of history to this source, who transcends from within the active and passive capacity of our freedom in the world to make history.

The christian's refusal to accept a universal subject of history has far-reaching consequences. On this basis, we would have to refuse to sacrifice one generation for the benefit of another—for example, the present generation in favour of the next. We are, however, also bound to conclude from this that the present generation and its established practices and structures cannot be an absolute norm. Ultimately too, the christian's view extends even into the past, with the result that not even the dead are excluded from the better world of the future. If we take the primacy of the future as our point of departure—and the first importance of the future is rightly emphasised nowadays—then we should not go so far as to make the demand for radical revolution legitimate: this would be a modern form of manicheanism, for which, in the social sphere, good and evil are irreconcilably opposed to each other. It is therefore already apparent that those philosophers and theologians who have rightly emphasised the primacy of the future have also begun to eliminate the rather menacing onesidedness of this idea by rehabilitating the past. E. Bloch, H. Marcuse, T. Adorno, P. Ricoeur and J. B. Metz have all in turn elaborated the idea of the 'past as a subversive memory'.

I am personally convinced that, on the basis of the same inner dynamics, the present has also to be rehabilitated, without denying the primacy of the future and, what is more, the present has to be rehabilitated in its critical power. If this is done, then it will be possible to reformulate in a very clear way the old problem which can be summed up in the contrast between Marx and Feuerbach; must we, like Feuerbach, aim at a revolution brought about by a 'conversion of the heart', a cultural revolution from which all the rest would follow, or should we, like Marx, aim at social and economic structural changes, from which all the rest would follow? Since the time of Marx, however, the situation has changed fundamentally and it has become clear from the different forms that the cultural revolution has assumed that the basic concern of the younger generations is not material or economic, but rather a preoccupation with 'personal liberation'. In America, for example, many of the younger critical spirits, who are inspired by marxism, are emphasising the priority of a 'new consciousness', because they are convinced that this will have an effect on politics and ultimately lead to a change in structures. On the basis of the change that has already taken place in the situation since the time that Marx was writing, these critics believe that their adaptation of Marx's insights is fully justified in the light of marxist principles. They therefore affirm that a cultural revolution necessarily precedes any structural change.

These American critics probably base their arguments too much on the contrast between Feuerbach and Marx in the sense outlined above, but the fact that radical movements are so often rendered impotent in a highly developed country such as the United States also plays a part in opening people's eyes to the reality of the situation. People are becoming more convinced that, in the West at least, only a cultural revolution, a 'new consciousness', can bring about a gradual change in the political situation and ultimately undermine and transform from within the Moloch of unfree structures. This idea has, of course, still to be worked out in detail, but it is already sufficiently clear for us to be able to ask seriously whether critical theory is not based on a contrast that has outlived its usefulness.

Despite the four objections outlined in the first part of this chapter, the fundamental inspiration of critical theory, especially as represented by Habermas, must be given due honour and it should certainly lead to an extension of hermeneutics. Truth, which is, of course, inwardly orientated towards universal agreement, also has a political dimension. The discovery of the truth presupposes structures which make this free consensus possible. In other words, truth presupposes maximally democratic structures. The discovery of the truth is therefore never a purely theoretical undertaking. Both the older and the new forms of hermeneutics have to be extended in a critical manner and, in view of the relationship between society and understanding, these hermeneutics must be inspired by a practical critical intention.

II Theology in correlation with a critical theory

The confrontation between the critical theory of society and actualising hermeneutic theology would have concluded with the discussion in the first part of this chapter, but for the fact that certain movements have recently made themselves felt in theological circles with what they call a new type of theology which include several elements of critical theory. I therefore propose to draw attention to various attempts to construct a critical theory from a definite theological option and to have this accepted as a new form of theology. This tendency is especially predominant among the younger generation throughout the world. It is certainly in no sense unanimous and its protagonists are trying to define it in various articles in critical christian journals, both protestant and catholic. Although it is, however, still too vague at present for it to be satisfacorily reduced to a common denominator, the major preoccupations of this new theology are already clear enough for us to be able to confront it with the classical hermeneutic theology, both in its conservative and in its progressive forms.

A. THE PROBLEM

There are at present two views, both claiming to be theology. On the one hand, there is the classical view of theology, which may be either conservative or progressive in its orientation. According to this view, theology is the continuation and making present of the church's interpretation of reality which began in the bible. Theology thus has a close and essential connection with faith and with the churches. It is possible to summarise the presuppositions of this essentially hermeneutic tradition in saying that the writings of the old and new testaments have primary and fundamental significance within the tradition of the church for the formation of theological theory.

On the other hand, however, there is another and more recent view of theology, according to which theology is bound to become a part of the critical theory of society. This option can be negatively defined as a criticism of the pathological 'hermeneutic circle' of the classical theory, that on the one hand the biblical text, as an external factor, acts as a norm for faith, whereas on the other hand the authority of this biblical text can only be understood and accepted in faith. This, however, is in conflict with the critical rationality which characterises every science, with the result that classical theology is by definition not a science, for those who hold this more recent view. The new theology can be positively defined as a science which is based on a rational, empirically deduced theory which can only be formulated after the results of religious sociology and psychology have been fully assimilated and worked out. It can therefore only emerge in conjunction with a theory of society which locates the social situation of faith and from this deduces the independent organisation of the church and theology. According to this view of theology, the churches are interpreted as an effective and socially therapeutic organisation which can make up for man's loss of identity in the consumer society of late capitalism. Some of the representatives of this theology have come to the conclusion that the classical view of theology as a hermeneutic science has to be rejected, because it is not a science, but an ideology.[105]

With this critical rationality, which is the hallmark of any science, in mind, we may now contrast these two positions. On the one hand, there is the view that theology is scientific on the basis of the christian message of faith and, on the other, there is the conviction that a theology which depends on faith and the church cannot be scientific and cannot lead to the formation of a theory.

B. CRITICISM OF THE CHURCH AS THE LEVER FOR CRITICISM OF
    SOCIETY

Several theologians who have become convinced of the validity of the critical thrust which emanates from the various critical theories of society are of the opinion that opposition to repressive and violent elements in our social structures should first be directed against the churches. These theologians believe that the churches play an essential part in reinforcing the aspect of compulsion in our social structures precisely because they are themselves 'great powers' in society.

It certainly cannot be denied that the church is in fact a political and social factor of considerable importance precisely because she is, from the social point of view, a great power. Theologians have often asked whether the church ought to intervene politically in certain circumstances, asking whether incidental and accidental intervention on the part of the church is in place, but forgetting the most important aspect of this question: that, as a great power in society, the church is already politically relevant. If, in other words, the church does not intervene in a given situation, this too is a political attitude, simply because the church is there as a social reality. It is clear from the sociological analyses that have been made that if elements of repression and violence are found in any society, the same elements will also be found in the churches, not by necessity, which would be in conflict with the idea of contingency in critical theory, but in fact. In view of the fact that the churches also use their faith, their *kerygma* and their *didache* ideologically, the church is, in the opinion of these theologians, the most obvious great power against which the lever of critical theory and praxis can be used in order to set the worldwide community of man free. The special aspect of this theological use of critical theory, then, is that emancipative opposition is first directed against the church so that, in the second place, the whole of society can be emancipated.

It is certainly true to say that the establishment always benefits enormously from a conservative church structure that resists change. It is not by accident that those who are most concerned about developments in the church are precisely those who want to preserve the established social and political order. A progressive, prophetic and emancipative church would be a major threat to their own positions and to the establishment in general, since the churches form a powerful part of society as a whole.

I do not feel qualified to analyse here the elements of repression and violence that are present in the structures of the catholic church. Familiarity with the church now and in the past shows that such elements exist, but only a scientific analysis would reveal how strong the alienating effect of these structures in the church really is. It should also not be forgotten that there is also a need to analyse specifically christian impulses to liberation evoked throughout history by the gospel as handed down to us in the church. If Habermas' theory that it is only in the modern era that it has become possible to construct a single history of man is in fact correct, there are in fact impulses which can only fully reveal their critical power in the social and political sphere on a worldwide scale in the modern age. It is consequently true to say that it is only in the modern age that social and political action on a hitherto unknown scale can in fact be evoked. This does not, however, mean that the churches are not included as great powers in late capitalist society and that they do not share in its repressive and violent structures. What is more, the point of departure taken by the churches in their official teaching about social order or the right to private ownership, for instance, is usually a capitalist view. This view is admittedly corrected to some extent by the churches, but it is not subjected to serious criticism as far as its presupposition, the basic right of capitalism, is concerned. Seen in this perspective, the church is undoubtedly an ideological structure accompanying and protecting the establishment.

C.   NOT THEOLOGY, BUT A FORM OF CRITICAL THEORY

The fact that these younger 'critical theologians' direct their attention in praxis first to the churches and then, via the churches, to society in general, is not in itself a reason for attributing to them a model of interpretation that is different from the one used by critical theory. There is, in other words, no reason for calling their scientific undertaking 'theology'. On the other hand, it is certainly possible to say that there is a convergence between the emancipative interest by which critical theory is guided, and the liberating power which proceeds from the gospel, although they are not identical. If it is authentically experienced, the christian message evolves its own specific form of freedom. This implies that the theologian who meditates on the implications of the gospel will also have specifically christian reasons for making critical theory, constitutively linked to a critical praxis, his own. In this sense, it is possible and correct to speak of critical catholicism or critical christianity. But if the same theologian makes use of critical theory and praxis because of a christian conviction this does not mean that critical theory is a theology. To convert it into a theology would be quite contrary to the original intention of critical theory itself. The simple fact that it is used by someone who is a theologian does not transform critical theory into a critical theology.

Yet it cannot be denied that the churches are also part of the social system and that, as such, they perform a special function within society. Like the sciences themselves,[106] the churches and the theology that is practised in them are not self-enclosed. They form an element within the social and economic system, the different processes of which are inwardly linked together. On the basis of this, every science, including theology, can be consciously or unconsciously used by 'the system' and, if this can be confirmed by analysis carried out on the basis of critical theory, the result is the detection of an uncritical form of theology. Theology is also part of the social complex and must therefore be included within the sphere which is analysed by critical theory and against which critical praxis can consequently be directed. Theology has therefore become the analysed and criticised (partial) object of the critical theory of society (which may be practised by the theologian himself). But even so, theologising itself is not part of critical theory. It is only the object of critical theory, even if that theory is practised by the theologian himself. In this sense, the critical theory of society is an auxiliary science at

the disposal of the theologian. It is therefore possible and even
necessary to take christianity and the churches as the object of
a historical and critical theory, just as it is also possible for
christianity, insofar as it is a social and psychological phenomenon, to be the object of study by those specialising in
psychoanalysis, cultural philosophy, religious sociology and
religious psychology.

Insofar as they are empirical data, religion, christianity and
the church all belong to those social forms the structure and
function of which merit specific analysis. A critical theory of
christianity can only be built up on the basis of analyses of
the historical forms in which it has appeared, and these can
be assessed scientifically. But even this does not mean that
the critical theory of christianity is a theology. What it shows,
however, is that theology, if it be regarded as a specific form
of theory (and this possibility cannot exclude critical theory,
which is implicitly based on hermeneutics) cannot be really
scientific, and therefore cannot really be theology, if it is not
consciously independent of present society. If theology is not
conscious of this need and has not assimilated critical theory
into its own design, it may well become an unscientific ideology.

Critical theory therefore certainly has the right to criticise
a hermeneutic theology which idealistically hypostasises its
object of research and reflection and give its social infrastructures no place in its considerations. This last question has
often been neglected by hermeneutic theology, even though
the results achieved by theology have been surprisingly good,
perhaps because it has, in the course of history, been very
sensitive, one might almost say naturally sensitive to man's
'sinful heart'. One is reminded here of the wisdom of the
East: 'however pure you may be, on your way you will finally
meet someone who is more pure and who will purify you'.
To this we might add that this saying applies both to the critic
of society and to the theologian.

D. THEOLOGY IS NOT TRACEABLE TO CRITICAL THEORY

In addition to critical theory, there are various other scientific
ways of approaching the phenomenon of christianity, one of
which is theology. I would describe theology in this context as
the scientific approach in which personal participation in
christian faith, as handed down within the churches, is so

effective that two positive results ensue. On the one hand, critical rationality and its accompanying scientific method is not amplified, supplemented or replaced in any way by any other method. On the other, the history of the christian interpretation of reality is continued and made actual in a spirit of creative loyalty and with a practical critical intent. According to this definition of theology as a scientific approach, christian faith is not something that is behind theology or can only be found in the theologian himself. On the contrary, it can be verified in theological activity. Theology is faith itself, if it is included in man's whole critical reflection.

In view of the fact that the critical theory of society takes hermeneutics as its implicit point of departure and has its own hermeneutic circle, those who accept and use this theory cannot deny *a priori* that theology, defined in this way as a science of faith and as a hermeneutic process, is really possible. Critical theory would in fact be going beyond its own scientific limits if it were to claim the right and the ability to decide whether it is *a priori* impossible to continue and to make present in real history the gospel of Christ.[107] An obvious consequence of critical theory is that an actualising theology, in which the christian interpretation is continued and made present, can only be justified if the spirit of the gospel is able to survive when subjected, as an ideology, to critical contestation and transformation. There is, however, no conceivable argument available for excluding *a priori* the possibility of the real continuation of the history of christian faith even when this has discarded the ideological form in which it now appears. Critical theory must take into account the possibility that christian faith can transcend its own ideological form in the future, so that it may appear to be much more than an ideology. If this possibility cannot be critically excluded— and it can be confirmed in the christian's own experience of the church's constant need of renewal—the protagonists of the critical theory of society at the same time cannot deny the legitimate status of theology as a separate hermeneutic approach to christian faith. These authors are bound to admit that theology cannot be traced back to critical theory or even to part of it. Even if they fail to acknowledge this, however, at least they cannot, on the basis of their own point of departure, exclude the possibility of a continuation and actualising of the christian interpretation of reality that is free from ideology.

E. THEOLOGY AS CORRELATIVE WITH CRITICAL THEORY

My claim that theology cannot be traced back to the critical theory of society or history does not bring the confrontation between the two to an end. This claim leads to the further assertion that, if the intention of the theology that continues and actualises the christian interpretation of reality is a practical, critical one, then theological hermeneutics are inevitably correlative with critical theory.

It is quite clear that, if such a theology remains tied to a purely theoretical form of hermeneutics and is not correlative with the critical movement of emancipative freedom, it can play no part in bringing about the history of the future. It will inevitably become a system of thought, confined to a decreasing minority of thinkers without any message of liberation for the world.

The relationship between theory and praxis as worked out by Habermas especially is, of course, of great importance to us if we want to understand correctly the hermeneutic process of this actualising theology. What is more, critical theory's understanding of itself as the self-consciousness of a critical praxis is also undoubtedly correct.

The theological process of making the apostolic faith present and actual in the world of today should not be a purely ideological process. There should, in other words, be a firm basis in history itself for the actualising interpretation of faith if this is to be at all credible. If this historical basis is overlooked, the process of making present will become purely speculative and theoretical and—as has so often happened—it will give the impression that all that theologians do is to make use afterwards of what has already been discovered and exploited.

The precondition for a credible theological process of continuing and actualising the christian message is that faith can still survive once its ideological framework has been broken down. In other words, the point of departure is that christianity is able to transcend the ideological form in which it appears, and that it can effect this transcendence in history, by means of a process that takes place in history. No attempt should be made to devise a new theology without first creating the sociological and therefore also ecclesiological conditions for that theology. The fact that such attempts are being made seems to me to constitute the crisis in which the churches are at present placed. In all such attempts, the essential empirical basis is lacking,[108] with the result that even the most enlightened efforts to renew theology are often little more than purely speculative ideology.

The theologian can, of course, defend himself, with good reason, against this charge, by pointing out that his experience is not confined to the contemporary church, but that it includes the past history of the church's life of faith. Although there is a good basis for this attitude, it is not entirely satisfactory because, despite the fact that it is certainly possible to find initiatives here and there in the past history of the church which correspond to what are now called movements of religious freedom, as a general rule the practice of the church in the past points in the opposite direction. Therefore, if we were now to speak, in an attempt to make the traditional christian teaching present and actual, of religious freedom as the teaching of the church, very many people would regard this as an unfair adaptation to the present situation and devoid of any basis in the past history of the church.

We can moreover also ask whether the theologian practises theology simply for himself, or simply perhaps for a handful of initiates. I have always been of the opinion that theology ought to be practised for the whole community of believers. These believers may have to trust the theologian's knowledge of scripture and tradition, but should they also trust his authority? What should at least be clear from these questions, however, is that theology is valueless, whether it is progressive or conservative, as soon as it loses contact with the empirical basis of the praxis of the community of believers.

If theology is, as I believe it ought to be, the self-consciousness of christian praxis, then it cannot, without coming to be regarded as an ideology tolerate a breach between a purely theoretical process of making present and a practical perpetuation and confirmation of earlier praxis. It is not the theologian who is the subject responsible for this process of making present, but the living community of believers. The theologian simply interprets critically their self-consciousness. Praxis, then, is an essential element of this actualising and liberating interpretation. In this sense, then, theology must be the critical theory (in a specifically theological manner) of the praxis of faith. Its point of departure is the contemporary praxis of the church. It analyses the models in which that praxis is presented and the attitudes on which it is based. In correlation with the critical theory of society, it also measures this praxis against its own evangelical claims and thus opens the way for new possibilities, which have, in turn, to be made a living reality in the praxis and faith of the church community. The relationship with praxis therefore forms an inseparable part of theological critical theory. What is more, the theologian, helped by his historical experience, has to express theoretically the theory that is implied in the new activities and patterns of behaviour of the believing community.

The necessary consequence of this situation and the necessary condition for it is that the believer can only identify himself partially with the empirical church. In the language of faith, it is certainly possible to call the church the 'body of the Lord', the 'temple of the Holy Spirit' or the 'community of God', but she is not the gospel, nor is she the kingdom of God, although she is the 'already' and the 'not yet' of these two realities. Even scripture is not the gospel. It is a historically conditioned, concrete form of the gospel, although it is, of course, the original form and, as such, the normative one. It is clear therefore that the gospel only allows us to identify ourselves partially with the empirical churches and that this identification at the same time includes the giving of the task to reform ourselves and the church until she begins to realise in praxis what she is proclaiming and confessing. The concept of 'ecclesiality', the reality of the church, has therefore to be used extremely carefully and subtly, and the difficulty is not solved by the introduction of such terms as the diaspora church, the anonymous church, the people's church, the voluntary church and so on.

Theology mediates between the two poles of scripture (or Christ) and the world, and has therefore to develop a form of criticism which is directed not only towards faith and the church, but also towards modern philosophy, which presupposes an interpretation of our humanity. This criticism is a theological criticism which is aware of the fundamentally unfathomable reality which is open to the mystery that strips reason, with its technical, communicative and critical praxis, of its ideological elements. When, for example, the group known as 'Kollektiv 17' asserts that the university is the place where the religious consciousness is subjected to methodical reflection and criticism, one is able to agree with this statement at once. When, however, this statement is followed by a further claim that 'the overcoming of religion must be understood as the practical consequence of academic training on the part of religiously motivated students of theology', then one is bound to ask whether what we have here is a case, not of a critical spirit, but of an emergent ideology. Without any attempt at self-justification, the critical theory claims to possess the universal status of a meta-theory which can act as the highest authority and pronounce judgements on the validity of religious talk and of actualising theology as defined in this chapter. The objection is sometimes made that christianity has not in fact changed the world, despite its actualising tendency, its constant self-renewal. This is clearly a very acute objection and it is not easy to give a precise yet sufficiently nuanced answer to it. On the other hand, it cannot be denied that christianity has brought about profound changes in many men's hearts. The fact that the world ought to have been changed by christian faith seems to have become an obvious conviction both in men's consciousness generally and in the consciousness of faith only relatively recently, and history, including the history of faith, is certainly a process of development. Just as a clear 'eternal reason' cannot be discovered in history, so too is it impossible to find an 'eternal faith' in it.

Christian redemption is certainly not something that takes place only in the hearts of individual men. It has both personal and social and political aspects, because it is man who is redeemed. It would, however, be simply a new ideology to expect the redemption and improvement of the world to come about automatically as the result of structural changes, which would remove all elements of repression and violence from society. Human freedom is situated in a context of external factors which influence that freedom. It is within this dialectical tension between interiority and exteriority, which must be seen not as a dualism but as a tense unity, that original sin as a datum of faith has to be situated and interpreted, and therefore also the datum of redemption, which would be fictitious if it did not attack the objective social structures which determine our lives.[109]

On the other hand, however, it would also be an illusion to believe in a redemption which might come about automatically because of new structures that were free of repression and violence. The redemption expected by christians implies an 'objective' redemption of this kind, but it also transcends it. Within the dialectical tension that exists between interiority and exteriority, outward structures will inevitably continue to be ambivalent. From the point of view of the philosophy of man, there must be a dialectical unity between man's inner conversion and the outward renewal of social, political and economic structures. A philosophical dualism here is certainly pernicious, but an ethical dualism can in no sense be excluded. Inner conversion can take place even in the most harsh social and political situations and a most profound state of injustice can prevail in men's hearts in a society with the least repressive and violent structures —an injustice which may lead to repression and violence, to domination of one's fellow-men.

In this respect, it is possible to speak of a mystical dimension in man's life and this implies that man can oppose repression and violence by giving meaning; in the face of his own impotence to change the objective structures at any given time, he can transcend the situation and affirm the meaning of real humanity. Even in the most apparently hopeless situation, there is always the possibility of mystical opposition through the sacrifice of the cross. This mystical form of criticism is, of course, not immune from possible misuse by the establishment. There are sufficient historical examples of the integration and neutralisation of the 'sacrifice of the cross' so that 'the system' will be perpetuated. In spite of this possibility of misuse, however, I am sure that the dialectical tension between the mystical dimension and the socio-political emancipative dimension is essential to the integrity of our humanity. This conviction is reinforced by the fact that the experience of freedom towards which critical theory is directed has by definition a 'theoretically hypothetical status'. In other words, it forms part of a world of ideas which is not dependent on what man is in actuality, with a situated freedom, a constitutive possibility of determining his fate in history. In view of the fact that man is situated in history, it would seem that the overcoming of every form of alienation is outside the realm of human possibility. For this reason, the mystical dimension, and also the liturgical dimension, are essential, so it would seem, to our humanity. They cannot be dismissed as a phenomenon left over from the past or as a form of compensation, if society still contains elements of repression and violence.

What theologians have learnt from critical theory is to be more cautious in their use of such terms as 'value', 'meaning' and 'peace'. These concepts seem positive enough, but their content has been indirectly or negatively deduced, with the result that theologians are reminded of the most distinctive characteristic of their science, namely that it is a *theologia negativa*. In our contemporary situation, however, this negative characteristic can be applied to a much wider sphere: for example, to the *polis*, the city of man with its disputed socio-political structures. Theologians are bound to speak in a much more negative way and their science must not only be purely theoretical; it must also function as the self-consciousness of a praxis. In this way, they will have to guarantee openness to the mystery and, without neglecting critical praxis, speak about it in parables. When scientific and critical analyses have been formulated in accordance with human reason, there always remains something meaningful that cannot be expressed rationally, but only in parables. There is indeed no better way of expressing the deepest mysteries of life. Jesus himself always spoke in parables because he wanted to say things that touched the very heart of our existence.

As Karl Rahner observed in a different context, theology is undoubtedly the *docta ignorantia futuri*.[110] Theology is not simply a criticism of a society which claims to be able to realise itself in the future purely on the basis of scientific and technological planning. It also has to criticise the critical theory of society which confidently expects salvation to come from critical negativity under the transcendental condition of what is possible and rational. This point of view can be affirmed and at the same time also transcended by religious and theological talk. It can be affirmed because, in our present situation, faith can only be appropriated critically. It can be transcended because faith expresses what is not irrational, but nonetheless transcends critical reasoning. Faith is distinguished by the fact that it is faith in what is humanly impossible. Reason and myth, critical rationality and faith are indispensable to each other. They protect each other from a degeneration into a complete ideological system which is bound to lead to repression and compulsion because it is self-enclosed and totalitarian. Critical theory therefore stimulates theology to investigate much more thoroughly the situations in which can be found what can be justifiably expressed in the language of faith and therefore in theological language. In this way, it is possible to avoid any appearance of ideology, since this is the consequence of statements that lack sufficient subtlety and which contain elements that compensate for a faulty social order.

F.   THE CRITICAL POWER OF KERYGMA AND DOGMA

It is only at critical periods in history that religious talk is concentrated into an explicit confession of faith in which the christian community seeks to distinguish itself from competing or alternative forms of religious talk. It was, for example, in such a critical situation that the community of believers had to formulate their faith in Christ through the form of a confession of original sin; in other words, they were at that time aware of their impotence themselves to bring about salvation and peace, both at the personal and at the collective level. The ideological presuppositions of this dogma can be understood in the light of the historically conditioned human sphere of understanding within which the dogma was defined. If, however, the dogma is stripped of its ideological framework, it may become what J. B. Metz has called, in a formula which he has applied to statements about faith in general, a 'subversive memory'.[111] In this case, the dogma of original sin reminds us of certain fundamental historical experiences, but does not imply that we have to return to the past. Above all, it represents, for christians, a criticism of the supporters of the critical theory of society, who tend to give a Pelagian interpretation to the emancipative praxis, regarding it as something that can always be achieved by purely human means. In itself, the dogma of original sin does not inevitably result in a conservative attitude, although it can be and indeed is misused in this way by the establishment. All that it claims to do now is to confront the advocates of critical theory with a critical question: can we really insist that man himself, on the basis of the critical theory with its emphasis on the unity of theory and praxis, can achieve a really emancipative history entirely and exclusively on his own initiative and power?

This confession of faith, the dogma of original sin, has, of course, to be verified critically against the analyses of Habermas and others. But is the 'theoretical hypothesis' of the critical theory equal to the reminder of danger in the dogma of original sin? Seen from the purely critical point of view, one is bound to say that only time will show whether this dogma of the critical theory is right. According to both, despite everything, the present situation is wrong. In conjunction with this condemnation of the present, critical theory maintains an 'optimism of reason' with regard to the future. This optimism of reason is not denied by the dogma of original sin, but insists that it is transcended in a pessimism that changes into an 'optimism of grace', in other words, redemption—redemption also for reason. In this way, the christian view, which is shared by all religions, is ultimately a correction of the over-optimism of critical theory. If, however, the christian language of faith, in this case the dogma of original sin, has a reactionary influence, it is clearly misdirecting its critical power. On the other hand, if its critical power is correctly used in christian praxis, it is possible for the dogma to confirm and at the same time to criticise the analyses of the critical theory. This possibility will, however, only be realised if a contemporary hermeneutic analysis of original sin is carried out in correlation with the critical theory of society.

If theologians do not give sufficient attention to these structural elements in their science, then they can expect to find the ideological remnants of theology confronted by the history of emancipative freedom. If, however, theologians analyse the language of their faith, in this case the dogma of original sin, they will have above all to express the constructive critical power of this dogma. This can be related to the datum that the idea of original sin only became a reality in the consciousness of christians in the light of Christ's redemption. Viewed in this way, the dogma is a confession, made in critical negativity, of the fact that the situation not only can, but also

must be different in Christ, and that this change takes place
within the history of man. It is therefore possible to say that
the dogma of original sin enshrines critical negativity, but
does this when this is situated within the positive sphere of
understanding of the promise, which has then to be constitutively linked to a christian praxis. This sphere of understanding is a promise for faith and love, which are made actual in
christian action as well as in christian prayer which, despite
its powerlessness, can and does move the world. In this way,
the christian confession of faith transcends the hypothetical
status of rational critical theory. In so doing, however, it
acts as the self-consciousness of critical christian praxis and is
based on God's grace.

III Towards a critical theology

On the basis of what has been said in the preceding section,
we may conclude that faith must continue to play an active
part in critical reflection, in other words, that faith calls for
a critical theology. This is so for two principal reasons.
1. In his search for the basis of his faith, the believer inevitably finds himself in a circle—he believes because he believes
and the 'why' of his act of faith can ultimately only be found
in that act itself, in the so-called *analysis fidei*.[112] This means
that different interpretations of faith are possible at levels
that are different from that of the act of faith. As a thinking
being, the believer therefore looks for other, similar interpretations and turns, for instance, to the psychology and sociology of religion. In every thinking person faith itself is
looking for a justification outside religion. This is the characteristic of every thinking believer. The jurisdiction of faith
is faith itself; in a sense, it is possible to say that the believer
does not know why he believes and, if he really knew why,
then faith would have dissolved. This does not mean, however,
that the search for a reason for faith is bound to take place
in an area to which criticism has no access. The certainty of
faith itself is, after all, to be found in an area in which it is
possible to justify it against all kinds of rational interpretation which cannot prove that the christian interpretation
is irrational or meaningless, since this interpretation cannot
be completely fathomed by reason alone.

The thinking christian is therefore in a situation of tension.

As a believer, he can only interpret his faith in a religious way but, as a thinking person, he has to try to interpret it in a non-religious way, since this is offered as a possibility to his thinking and since it also plays a part in his being a believer. This is clear from the findings of the various sciences that are concerned in different ways with religion: psychology, psychoanalysis, sociology and the critical theory, for example. P. Ricoeur's formulation of the problem of the pluriformity of interpretations was very clear,[113] and he at least questioned the way in which they are in conflict with each other and the possible ways in which a reconciliation may be effected. The believer cannot, moreover, deny the validity of non-religious interpretations of faith, nor can he simply affirm its validity: faith is, after all, something quite different. If he were to do so, he would be moving perilously close to the position of positivism with regard to faith and revelation.

It is clear from a philosophical consideration of our humanity in the context, for instance, of the evolutionary view of the world, that there is a difference between the way any human conviction comes into being and the eventual reasons for that conviction. Similarly, the way in which we come to the point of believing and the reason why we believe are not the same. The development of faith can be analysed with the help of psychology, sociology and critical theory, for instance, but this rational process does not ultimately reveal precisely what the source of faith and our reason for believing are. In scientific analysis, the active subject of these objective expressions of man in society has always to be presupposed. It is not as such involved in it. The sciences do not in any sense create man in the world, with all his social, ethical and religious aspects; this is a datum which precedes scientific analysis, and forms its point of departure. This presupposed datum impels us to investigate critically the source of faith and the reason for believing.[114] The objectivised aspect of man investigated by the sciences is not, however, the whole man. It is clear from philosophical reflection that the full reality of man's being is not exhausted by scientific analysis and indeed this very reflection itself shows that man cannot be identified with the aspect of him that is objectivised in history and examined scientifically. Man himself transcends all scientific interpretations and this is precisely why he has always achieved unexpected and unhoped for things in history and will always be able to go beyond these, achieving even greater things in the future.

This human possibility of self-transcendence is, of course, an unfathomable mystery which cannot be identified with what science has discovered or will discover about man. There is therefore a possibility of interpretation in depth, which attempts to fathom the reason for this self-transcendence and looks for a freedom which makes purely human freedom possible and which forms its basis. According to christian faith, the ultimate reason for this human self-transcendence, which cannot be fully grasped by scientific study, is to be found in the transcendence of God who, in a transcendent yet inward manner, enables man to go beyond what he has already accomplished and move towards what he hopes for and what has been promised to him. In other words, man is able, by virtue of the divine transcendence within him, to transcend the 'already' and strive towards the 'not yet'. The possibility and the meaningfulness of this interpretation of christian faith cannot be disproved by scientific methods or models of interpretation. Science has therefore to leave this possibility open.

2. The second reason why faith requires a critical theology is this. There is, in christian faith, a tension between that part of God's promise that has already been fulfilled and the part that we still hope for, in other words, between the 'already' of realised eschatology and the 'not yet' of future eschatology. Christian faith is in the middle of a history in which eschatology is being realised. In the bible, both the old and the new testaments, the question of meaning is treated as a question about the ultimate meaning of history. The precise content of this ultimate meaning is not given to us in scripture in any positive form. What we have are negative, evocative symbols, such as a kingdom without tears, misery or alienation. Because of our faith in Christ, we have been promised that this ultimate meaning can indeed be realised as a redeeming possibility and as something to be done.

It is therefore possible to say that theology, as a critical and rational reflection about faith, works with a hypothesis which is the thesis of faith: the meaning that is given in the bible not only can be made present and actual again and again in history, but also must and will be actualised in this way. In the course of history, this hypothesis must be tested, and we must also remain open to the possibility that it will be falsified rather than proved true, especially if the attempt to make the meaning of the bible present in history is definitively abandoned. Seen in this light, it should be clear that the theologian does not begin with the hypothesis that constant progress is assured, but bases himself rather on the presupposition that it is not impossible to give a meaning to history, however ambiguous it may be, and therefore that the attempt to do so should never be abandoned. At the same time, he recognises that, as a theologian, he is not in a position to formulate any principle, either theoretically or practically, which might include the whole of human history. It is this that distinguishes christian theology from both Hegel's and Marx' view of history, leaving out of account, of course, the contemporary movement to re-interpret the work of these two thinkers.

It is clear, then, that both defeatist interpretations of history and interpretations which take as their theoretical or practical point of departure a total meaning that has previously been established as certain, even if only in a utopian manner, are therefore bound to be subject to the criticism of christian faith. There is no area safe from criticism, not even for faith.[115] The meaning that is communicated to us in the historical event of revelation is not a tautologous system that is above history: faith too shares in the ambivalence that is common to everything historical, just as Jesus himself shared in the disputable character that characterises the history of man. (This is, of course, the reason why non-christian interpretations of the christian revelation are fully justified.) There is consequently an inner connection between man's consciousness of faith and his historical and critical consciousness. This is, for example, clear from the way in which the members of the 'New Quest' movement have renewed the quest for the historical Jesus and from the possibility of approaching scripture in accordance with form criticism and traditio-historical methods.[116] The answer that the bible gives us to our fundamental question about meaning is to offer us an interpretation of history which is made in faith, but is at the same time critical in that it is distinguished from other interpretations. Since the christian interpretation is also situated in history, it has to be permanently and consistently continued in critical thought. This is required by faith itself, because it is open to criticism, although it cannot be undermined by criticism. Criticism is able to demonstrate that other interpretations of christian faith do not have to be entirely without foundation. It can, however, also show that the christian interpretation of history is not without foundation. Although it is not the only interpretation that can be justified, it certainly can be justified by reason. This is a situation that is based in the ambiguity of history itself.

If this is properly understood, it should be clear in which direction a dogmatic theology that is also critical should be worked out. It must begin with the question of the meaning of history. This will mean that themes such as redemption and the significance of Christ and the church will be discussed within the eschatological sphere. The critical and hermeneutic contribution that the theologian can make to the present and future praxis of the church is above all an understanding of the past and an attempt to make it actual and present, so that we can discover, in our present situation, the direction that we should follow in living for the future.

Theology is the critical self-consciousness of christian praxis in the world and the church. If we take this as our point of departure, then it seems to me that we should not be alarmed by the fact that the theologian is nowadays, as he has always to some extent been in the past, often suspected both by those who uphold the primacy of reason and by (uncritical) believers who insist on the primacy of faith. In the eyes of both groups of people, the theologian apparently denies the interpretation of reality which they advocate, so that he has to be regarded as heretical. The critical science of faith, which theology aims to be, is therefore condemned as heretical both by faith and by reason. But this is precisely the irreplaceable contribution which both faith and reason can make to the interpretation of reality, insofar as both tend inevitably to perpetuate themselves in establishing a system. The theologian is therefore the custodian of transcendence, but he does not guard it like a treasure. On the contrary, he prevents it from becoming a datum, because he is conscious of the fact that transcendence must be won again and again in the face of historical alienation and must therefore always be kept in mind in any critical praxis. Theology is the critical theory

of the critical praxis which has this intention and it therefore does not hesitate to use the meaning and nonsense that
have been discovered in man and society by the human,
analytical and hermeneutic sciences. It will probably be clear,
then, that theology without faith simply produces nonsense
and is therefore the opposite of theology, although this does
not mean that it cannot achieve positive results at a different
level. At the same time, it should also be clear that faith without theology is hardly worthy of the name of faith.

NOTES

The Understanding of Faith is a translation of *Geloofsverstaan* with the omission of chapters 1 and 7 which were translated in *God the Future of Man*. The other chapters have been renumbered accordingly, so Dutch 2–6 become English 1–5 and 8–9 become 6–7.

1. See my *Revelation and Theology*, London and Sydney 1967, especially pp 69–92, in which the development of dogma in modern times is discussed. Even then, I preferred to speak of the development of tradition, because this development is not purely theoretical. In this I was influenced by the thought of Maurice Blondel.

2. A full critical *exposé* is impossible here, but the following is an illustration. In the national-religious epic of the book of Joshua we read: 'Called and mightily helped by our God Joshua entered upon the land at the head of the twelve tribes and conquered all of it, after which each tribe was allotted its own territory. Thus God fulfilled all his promises, not one was unfulfilled' (Jos 21:45). Here a past (somewhat different here from what actually happened) was re-interpreted and this interpretation became at the same time an expression of a new belief in national restoration after the Assyrians had destroyed the realm of the ten northern tribes in 721. When, after 650, Assyrian power began to wane, Israel's hope of an untroubled possession of the 'whole of Yahweh's land' revived. This book, written under King Josiah, 640–609, and recast during the exile, thus describes the past from the angle of a new hope of the future, the signs of which were seen in contemporary events.

3. This shows that the schema of 'promise and fulfilment', as developed, for instance, by J. Moltmann (*The Theology of Hope* London 1966), can only be understood if we presuppose a conception of history as 'history of the transmission of traditions' as elaborated by W. Pannenberg in his many works, particularly since he has abandoned this schema of 'promise and fulfilment' in order

to put more weight on the continuity of the history of traditions. See *Theology as History* (vol 3 of *New Frontiers in Theology* New York Evanston and London 1967), pp 252ff, with nn 60, 61 and 69.

4. O. Procksch *Theologie des Alten Testaments* (Gütersloh 1950), p 591; G. von Rad 'Basileia' in *Theologisches Wörterbuch zum Neuen Testament*, I (Kittel), pp 566f; T. Vriezen *Hoofdlijnen der Theologie van het Oude Testament* (Wageningen ³1966).

5. V. Maag 'Malkût Jhwh' in *Supplements to Vetus Test* 7 (1960), pp 129–153.

6. 'The Hermeneutics of Eschatological Assertions' in *Theological Investigations* IV (London 1966), p 150.

7. See, for example, Dallas High *Language, Persons and Belief* New York 1969; see also *New Essays on Religious Language*, edited by Dallas High, New York 1969.

8. This is true in the widest sense even of formal language games such as logic and mathematics: but I need not go into this here.

9. For the doxological aspect of the *kerygma* and of dogma, see especially E. Schlink *Der kommende Christus und die kirchliche Tradition* Göttingen 1961, pp 24–79; W. Pannenberg *Grundfragen systematischer Theologie* Göttingen 1967, pp 158–201. For a linguistic analytical approach to the problem of the logic of doxological speaking, see Lars Bejerholm and G. Hornig *Wort und Handlung: Untersuchungen zur analytischen Religionsphilosophie* Gütersloh 1966.

10. When Thomas Aquinas, for instance, asked whether Christ had an *intellectus agens*, the theological relevance of this depended on the consistency of this idea with regard to Christ's humanity, viewed within the model of his own elaboration of Aristotelian philosophy of man. His doctrine of the *intellectus agens* is not given a religious meaning or a theological relevance because of this.

11. See my *Mission of the Church* London 1973, ch 1, pp 1–19.

12. W. Pannenberg (ed) *Offenbarung als Geschichte* Göttingen 1961ff; *ibid Grundfragen systematischer Theologie* Göttingen 1967; *ibid Theologie als Geschichte* (*Neuland in der Theologie* III), edited by J. Robinson and J. Cobb, Zürich 1967; see also I. Berten *Histoire, Révélation et Foi. Dialogue avec W. Pannenberg* Brussels 1969.

13. See, for example, F. de Saussure *Cours de linguistique générale* Paris 1963; B. Malmberg *Les nouvelles tendances de la linguistique* Paris 1966 (originally written in Swedish); E. Benveniste *Problèmes de linguistique générale* Paris 1966; *ibid Langage* Paris 1967; A. J. Greimas *Sémantique structurale* Paris 1966; J. Piaget *Le structuralisme* Paris 1968; G. Schiwy, *Der französische Strukturalisme* Hamburg 1969; James Barr *The Semantics of Biblical Language* London

1961; *ibid Old and New in Interpretation* London 1966; *ibid Biblical Words for Time* London 1966; P. Ricoeur 'Contribution d'une réflexion sur le langage à une théologie de la Parole' in *Revue Théol Phil* (Lausanne) 18 1968, pp 333–348; Robert W. Funk *Language, Hermeneutic and Word of God* New York 1966.

14. C. A. van Peursen *Fenomenologie en analytische filosofie* Hilversum 1968; W. Stegmüller *Hauptströmungen der Gegenwartsphilosophie* Stuttgart 1965³; H. G. Gadamer, *Wahrheit und Methode* Tübingen 1960ff; R. Kwant *Fenomenologie van de taal* Utrecht 1963; O. Loretz and W. Strolz (eds) *Die hermeneutische Frage in der Theologie* Freiburg 1968; G. Gusdorf *La Parole* Paris 1956; M. Merleau-Ponty *Phénoménologie de la perception* Paris 1945; see also *Signes* Paris 1960, II, 'Sur la phénoménologie du langage', pp 105–122.

15. Benvéniste *op cit*, p 130.

16. J. Royce *The Problem of Christianity* New York 1911; elaborated by C. K. Ogden and I. A. Richards in *The Meaning of Meaning* New York 1933; see also Malmberg *op cit*, pp 187–188.

17. J. Macquarrie *God-Talk: An Examination of the Language and Logic of Theology* New York and London 1967, pp 55–78.

18. Gadamer *op cit*, pp 289–290; see also G. Stachel *Der neue Hermeneutik* Munich 1967, p 32.

19. *Unterwegs zur Sprache* Pfullingen 1959, p 275.

20. See I. T. Ramsey *Religious Language* London 1957 and *Models and Mystery* London 1964.

21. See, for example G. Nuchelmans *Proeven van een analytisch filosoferen* Hilversum 1967; J. Urmson *Philosophical Analysis* Oxford 1956; J. Martin *The New Dialogue between Philosophy and Theology* London 1966; A. Flew and A. McIntyre (eds) *New Essays in Philosophical Theology* London ²1966; F. Ferré *Language, Logic and God* New York 1961; A. J. Ayer *Language, Truth and Logic* New York ²1946.

22. See especially I. T. Ramsey, *op cit*.

23. *Unterwegs zur Sprache, op cit*; *Was heiss Denken?* Tübingen 1954; *Einführung in die Metaphysik* Tübingen ³1966; *Vom Wesen der Wahrheit* Frankfurt 1954ff; *Gelassenheit* Pfullingen 1959ff; *Holzwege* Frankfurt ³1957; see also O. Pöggeler *Der Denkweg M. Heideggers* Pfullingen 1963; Auke de Jong *Een wijsbegeerte van het woord* Amsterdam 1966; S. Ijsseling *Heidegger, Denken en danken* Antwerp 1964; H. Noack *Sprache und Offenbarung* Gütersloh 1960.

24. Although my point of view is fundamentally inspired by W. Pannenberg here and is quite remote from that of Ogden, I have been guided by the American version and the corrected translation of Bultmann made by Schubert Ogden in his book, *The Reality of God and Other Essays* London 1967.

25. The interrelationship between the universal revelation of being in the word and the unique christian revelation expressed in the church—these two revelations reinforcing each other and making each other intelligible—also throws light on the problem of the so-called question-answer correlation and points the way to a possible solution to this problem (see ch 5).

26. John Hick *Faith and Knowledge* New York 1957.

27. No one has analysed this confrontation more clearly or done more to bring it about than K. O. Apel; see his contributions to Loretz and Strolz, *op cit* note 12, pp 86–155; in *Welterfahrung in der Sprache* Freiburg 1968, pp 9–28; in *Zeitschrift für Theologie und Kirche* 63 (1966) pp 49–87; and *Philosophisches Jahrbuch* 75 (1967) pp 56–94. See also C. A. van Peursen *Fenomenologie en analytische filosofie, op cit* note 12. It should be noted in this connection, however, that whereas Apel confronts linguistic analysis with Heidegger's hermeneutical ontology, van Peursen confronts it only with phenomenology.

28. In Loretz and Strolz p 148.

29. *Ibid*, p 150.

30. This aspect of the priority of the word of God has been analysed very well by J. Ratzinger in his *Einführung in das Christentum* Munich 1968, pp 61–66.

31. P. van Buren *The Secular Meaning of the Gospel* New York 1963, especially pp 159–168.

32. A good criticism of this existential interpretation, which at the same time preserves its essential affirmation, will be found in L. Bakker's 'Orthodoxie en vrijzinnigheid. De zin van het thematiseren en dogmatiseren van het geloof' *Jaarboek 1967/68 Werkgenootschap kath theol Nederland* Hilversum 1968, pp 121–185. 'In the new self-understanding, the act by which it is called to mind is always *co-understood*' (p 131). Without this last statement, the progressive, liberal attitude is a-dogmatic and unchristian.

33. See H. Fortmann *Geloof bij kenterend getij* Roermond and Maaseik 1968, p 135; this idea has been elaborated by B. Willems *De verlossing in kerk en wereld* Roermond and Maaseik 1967.

34. P. Munz has called a community that is built up on one theology the definition of a schism; see *Problems of Religious Knowledge* London 1959, p 177.

35. *Philosophical Investigations* I, § 197 ff; see N. Malcolm 'Wittgenstein's Philosophical Investigations' *Philosophical Review* 63 (1954), pp 530–559.

36. This expression is J. Royce's, based on C. S. Peirce. See especially J. Royce *The Problem of Christianity* New York 1911. For the background to their pragmatism, see A. J. Ayer *The Origins of Pragmatism* London 1968.

37. Although I find this question posed by the analytical philosophers personally sympathetic, I do not wish to associate myself with their generally anti-metaphysical presupposition. It should, however, be noted that analytical philosophy—a philosophy which, basing itself on logical and linguistic analysis, has developed techniques by means of which theological questions and answers also can be verified against their meaningfulness or meaninglessness— is not in itself anti-metaphysical. This is clear, for example, from R. C. Hinners *Ideology and Analysis. A Rehabilitation of Metaphysical Ontology* Bruges and New York 1961, and *Prospects for Metaphysics*, ed Ian T. Ramsey New York 1961, quite apart from the works of Ramsey himself.

38. 'Historiciteit en interpretatie van het dogma' *Tijdschrift voor Theologie* 8 1968, p 307.

39. See J. Hick *Faith and Knowledge* New York (Ithaca) 1957.

40. For the concept 'intelligible structure', see J. P. Jossua, 'Immutabilité, progrès, ou structurations multiples des doctrines chrétiennes' *Revue des sciences philosophiques et théologiques* 52 1968, p 173–200.

41. See J. P. Jossua *op cit*, p 185. R. van Iersel also speaks about models of interpretation'. See, for example, his article 'Interpretatie van de schrift en van het dogma' in *Tijidschrift voor Theologie* 8 1968, especially pp 324–326.

42. See B. Schillebeeckx *Revelation and Theology* London and Melbourne 1967, pp 10–11.

43. See *Kerygma und Mythos* Hamburg 1952, (2) p 188; see also *Jesus Christus und die Mythologie* Hamburg 1964, p 63.

44. 'Where this is successful, it can only be a gain for philosophical thought, insofar as more than a negative dialectic, which marks off the limits of the finite and of all available realisation of meaning, is involved in it. In other words, the illumination of a sphere of meaning which constantly guides such a negative dialectic and which is previously given to all subjective assumption, but which only enters the available world by an act of freedom on the part of the subject . . .'; see W. Pannenberg, 'Christliche Theologie und philosophische Kritik' *Revue de Théologie et de Philosophie* Lausanne 18 1968, p 371. Pannenberg concludes his article with these words, but does not elaborate the statement which I have quoted and which I believe to be important. I try to do this in broad outline here.

45. From the logical point of view, of course, it is not possible to speak meaningfully about God on the basis of a view of language which can and does only aim to express empirically verifiable reality. It should be noted, however, that more than one positivist does accept religion in the form of a silence about the inexpressible, a silence 'accompanied by parable'; see especially T. Mc-

Pherson, 'Religion as the Inexpressible', *New Essays in Philosophical Theology* ed A. Flew and A. McIntyre London [5]1966, pp 131–143; R. Miles, *Religion and the Scientific Outlook* London 1959. According to this hypothesis, it is also, from the logical point of view, equally impossible to speak meaningfully about the unique and absolute significance of the one man Jesus. If the believer does this, he is certainly acting illogically, but he is fully acting as a christian. This is also clear from P. van Buren's subtle exposition in *Theological Explorations*. Despite the rejection of any doctrine about God, it is possible to discern here something of the Reality for which every name, even that of 'transcendence', is inadequate. Van Buren is not a neo-positivist. I prefer to regard him as an analytical 'open pragmatist' who acknowledges that the christian view of life has as much right to exist as all other interpretations of reality, but who cannot make this option rationally true except in practice and in the later judgement of history.

46. See John Macquarrie *God-Talk. An Examination of the Language and Logic of Theology* New York 1967 especially chapter 3, pp 55–78. Cf also note 34.

47. P. Ricoeur, 'Tasks of the Ecclesial Community in the Modern World' *Theology of Renewal* Toronto 1968 part 2, pp 252–253.

48. *Lumen Gentium* 28 and *Ad Gentes* 20.

49. From the ecclesiological point of view, it therefore gives an unhealthy impression when believers, who are assumed to say or sing the creed liturgically at least once a week, are required to make further professions of faith when they accept office in the church. Is this not a devaluation of the principle of *lex orandi, lex credendi,* when every possible benefit is expected to come from a juridical oath, in other words, when the emphasis is not placed on the prayer of the profession of faith and the liturgical 'amen', but only on the added juridical obligations?

50. See, for example, Ian T. Ramsey *Religious Language* London 1957, pp 158–179, and even more clearly, S. Laeuchi *The Serpent and the Dove: Five Essays on Early Christianity* London 1966.

51. *Dei Verbum* 10.

52. B. van Iersel, 'Interpretatie van de schrift en van het dogma', *Tijdschrift voor Theologie* 8 1968, p 326; K. Rahner 'Was ist eine dogmatische Aussage?' *Schriften zur Theologie* 5 Einsiedeln 1962, especially pp 67–72.

53. P. Schoonenberg *op cit,* p 309.

54. *Identität und Differenz* Pfullingen 1957, p 51.

55. *Die Existenz Gottes im Bekenntnis des Glaubens* Munich 1963.

56. *Systematic Theology* London 1953.

57. *Wort und Glaube* Tübingen 1960, p 365.

58. *Wort und Glaube op cit* pp 364–365.

59. Paris 1956; see also P. Ricoeur's review of this book in *Esprit* 25 1957 nos 7–8, p 124–135.

60. *Eléments pour une Ethique* Paris 1962.

61. 'The Doctrine of God and Man in the Theology of Bultmann' *The Theology of Bultmann* New York 1966, pp 83–103.

62. A good summary will be found in A. Wellmer *Kritische Gesellschaftstheorie und Positivismus* Frankfurt 1969, pp 45–44.

63. Wellmer *op cit* pp 54–55.

64. H. D. Bahr *Kritik der 'politischen Technologie'* Frankfurt and Vienna 1970; *ibid Die Linke antwortet Habermas* Frankfurt 1968.

65. J. Habermas *Theorie und Praxis* Neuwied ³1969, p 289.

66. Habermas *Theorie und Praxis op cit* pp 245–246.

67. J. Habermas *Erkenntnis und Interesse* Frankfurt 1968, pp 143–178; *ibid Technik und Wissenschaft als 'Ideologie'* Frankfurt 1968, pp 148–149, 155–157.

68. *Erkenntnis und Interesse*, pp 178–233; *Technik und Wissenschaft*, pp 157–158.

69. This is the theme which dominates the whole of Habermas' *Zur Logik der Sozialwissenschaften* Tübingen 1967; see also *Technik und Wissenschaft*, pp 149–150, and especially pp 155–159.

70. 'Transcendental' is used here not in the classical philosophical sense or in the Kantian sense, but in a post-Kantian sense. It points to conditions which cannot be overlooked and which are therefore valid in all situations prevailing in social life.

71. *Technik und Wissenschaft*, p 164.

72. *Erkenntnis und Interesse*, p 259.

73. *ibid*, pp 262–299.

74. There are certain objections to this model; see P. Ricoeur *De l'interprétation. Essai sur Freud* Paris 1965.

75. See especially M. Xhaufflaire *Feuerbach et la théologie de la sécularisation* Paris 1970.

76. See Wellmer *op cit*, pp 61 ff.

77. C. B. McPherson *The Political Theory of Possessive Individualism* Oxford 1962.

78. *Theorie und Praxis*, p. 289: 'The dependence of criticism on science and on empirical, historical, sociological and economic analyses is so inescapable that it can only be refuted, within theory, scientifically'.

79. *Erkenntnis und Interesse*, pp 332–364; Wellmer, *op cit*, pp 52–53.

80. *Theorie und Praxis*, pp 213–214.

81. *Theorie und Praxis op cit*, p 213.

82. Xhaufflaire *Feuerbach op cit*, p 287; here Xhaufflaire follows Habermas.

83. *Theorie und Praxis,* pp 213–214: 'Man has never before been so inescapably confronted with the ironical fact that he can himself make history, even though it still to a great extent lies outside his control, since the development of so many means of violent self-assertion, the effects of which make their use as a means of achieving certain political aims very open to doubt.'

84. *Theorie und Praxis,* p 289.

85. Wellmer *op cit,* p 42.

86. *Theorie und Praxis,* p 214.

87. For criticism on the basis of a scientific analysis, see *Theorie und Praxis,* pp 289, 171 etc.

88. *Theorie und Praxis,* p 214.

89. *ibid* especially the appendix.

90. The term 'ideology' has many different meanings. It was first used in the discussion between members of the French enlightenment and Napoleon; see Werner Post, 'Ideologie' *Sacramentum Mundi* VI Bussum 1969, pp 71–76. The unfavourable senses in which the term is used nowadays predominate to such a degree that it would only give rise to misunderstandings if the more favourable senses were stressed. For the various meanings of 'ideology', see H. G. Gadamer 'Rhetorik, Hermeneutik und Ideologiekritik' *Kleine Schriften* I Tübingen 1967, pp 113–130; J. Habermas 'Die Universalitätsanspruch der Hermeneutik' *Hermeneutia und Dialektik* I Tübingen 1970, pp 73–104; K. O. Apel 'Szientistik, Hermeneutik, Ideologiekritik' *Wiener Jahrbuch für Philosophie* I 1968; Helm 'Die Universalitätsanspruch der Hermeneutik' *Hermeneutik und Dialektik op cit* I, pp 343–356; K. Lenk (ed) *Ideologie, Ideologiekritik und Wissenssoziologie* Neuwied ³1967; P. Berger and T. Luckmann *Die gesellschaftliche Konstruktion der Wirklichkeit* Stuttgart 1969, pp 132–138; K. Mannheim *Ideology and Utopia* London 1936; G. Picht *De toekomst in eigen hand* Baarn 1970; W. Dirks, 'Gottesglaube und Ideologiekritik' *Wer ist das eigentlich – Gott?* Munich 1969, pp 220–231. In the terminology of the critical theory of society, 'ideology' means a false consciousness or a speculative assertion for which no empirical or historical basis can be provided and which therefore has a broken relationship with reality.

91. Xhaufflaire *op cit,* p 289.

92. Habermas' *Seminarthesen* (14 December 1968) and his *Erklärung vor Studenten* (12 December 1968) are to be found in his *Protestbewegung und Hochschulreform* Frankfurt 1969, pp 245–248, 244–245.

93. *loc cit,* pp 244–248.

94. This only applies to those critics, such as H. Marcuse, who regard man as basically a creature of impulse. Habermas is cer-

tainly not one of these. He regards emancipative freedom as the fundamental concern of human reason (*Vernunft*) and this is not an option, but the result of philosophical analysis. It is therefore possible to ask why the rational project of truth, which is certainly liberating, is just as fundamental a concern of human reason as is emancipation. The fact that Habermas confines himself to emancipation as such must ultimately be called a fundamental option.

95. See A. Wellmer *Kritische Gesellschaftstheorie und Positivismus* Frankfurt 1969, and the article 'Unpolitische Universität und Politisierung der Wissenschaft' in J. Habermas *Protestbewegung und Hochschulreform* Frankfurt 1969, pp 249–258.

96. A. Wellmer *op cit*, p 51.

97. See my article 'Het nieuwe Godsbeeld, secularisatie en politiek' *Tijdschrift voor Theologie* 8 (1968), p 57 ff, 3 and 'Het officiëel-kerkelijk spreken over sociaal-politieke toekomstproblemen' *Concilium* 4 (1968) 6, pp 21–40.

98. The title of a book by the French philosopher G. Bachelard Paris ³1962.

99. See my article 'Towards a Catholic Use of Hermeneutics' *God the Future of Man* London and Sydney 1969, especially pp 14–15, note 20 (pp 46–47) and above pp 63–70.

100. M. Heidegger *Sein und Zeit* Halle (1927) 1953, para 32, especially pp 152–153.

101. H. Marrou *De la connaissance historique* Paris ⁴1959 in which the author speaks of a 'spiral' and an 'ellipse'; R. Hart *Unfinished Man and the Imagination* New York 1968, especially pp 52–68.

102. This was said by A. Wellmer *Kritische Gesellschaftstheorie,* p 52, in a correct diagnosis of this model of interpretation.

103. See my report to the congress held in September 1970 under the auspices of *Concilium,* 'Het kritisch statuut van de theologie', published in *De toekomst van de kerk. Verslag van het wereldcongres Concilium te Brussel* Amersfoort and Bussum 1970, pp 56–64.

104. J.-B. Metz *Reform und Gegenreformation heute* Mainz 1969, p 15.

105. See especially W. Huber, W. Trillhaas, K. Altner, R. Lindner and the so-called 'Kollektiv 17' in *Evangelische Kommentare* 2 (1969) no 4, pp 207ff, 209–210, 219–221, 230–233; no 5, pp 279ff. Similar views have been expressed in such movements as 'Kritischer Katholizismus' and 'Tegenspraak' ('Contestation').

106. For the social functions of the sciences and the universities, see especially A. Wellmer *Unpolitische Universität op cit.*

107. Unlike many other authors who advocate critical theory, M. Xhaufflaire has explicitly admitted that theology cannot be traced

back to the critical theory of history; see his *Feuerbach et la théologie de la sécularisation* Paris 1970, p 300.

108. The exegete F. J. Schierse has said, for example: 'Even in the early church, theology was above all reflection about experiences of faith on the part of individuals and the community. Nowadays, the church must first of all be reorganised in such a way that its message and the reason for its presence in the world is once again made clearly visible in the form in which it appears. ... When this happens, recent theological knowledge will emerge spontaneously as the result of christian experience in faith'; see his *Was hat die Kirche mit Jesus zu tun?* Düsseldorf 1969, p 25; cf also: 'The existential preconditions must first be created in the church if the christian message is to be interpreted in a new and better way' *ibid*, p 32.

109. This could be called an 'objective redemption', but in this case the term would have a meaning that is quite different from the traditional meaning.

110. 'Die Frage nach der Zukunft', *Diskussion zur 'politischen Theologie'* Mainz and Munich 1969, pp 247–266; see also R. Popper 'Selbstbefreiung durch Wissen' L. Reinisch (ed) *Sinn der Geschichte* Munich 1967, p 109.

111. In his postscript to *Diskussion zur 'politischen Theologie' op cit*, especially pp 284–296.

112. Thomas Aquinas ultimately based the certainty and the real criterion of faith—rightly, in my opinion—in what he calls 'the light of faith'. The *motivum fidei* is, thanks to the grace of faith, to be found *in* the act of faith. This *motivum fidei* must be strictly distinguished from the *motiva credibilitatis* because such motives are situated at a different level, namely that of the morally justified and free use of human reason. I can only give consent to the 'why' of my faith *in faith* and this cannot be completely fathomed simply by a use of reason; it is equally true to say that the act of faith is rationally unjustified. This is, of course, the fundamental idea of his treatise on faith. The theologians who followed Cajetan misunderstood the original Thomist view, with the result that his teaching about the light of faith disappeared from theology altogether until the beginning of the present century, when it was rediscovered by the school of Le Saulchoir on the one hand (Gardeil and Chenu) and P. Rousselot on the other.

113. *Le conflit des interprétations. Essai d'herméneutique* Paris 1969.

114. As Peter Berger has so rightly said, sociologists study religion as a human projection, based on specific infra-structures of human history. He also insists, correctly in my opinion, that the content of christianity must, like that of every other religious tradition, be analysed as a human projection. It is also only after he has

really understood what it means to say that religion is a human product or projection, Berger claims, that the sociologist can look, within this field of projections, for what may seem to be signals of transcendence. See Berger's book *Het hemels baldakijn* Utrecht 1969, pp 198, 104 and 206. (ET *The Sacred Canopy*.)

115. If the motive of faith, that cannot be rationally fathomed—traditionally the *lumen quo* of faith—can be called a 'safe area', then there certainly is such an area in faith. This is, however, in my opinion, a wrong use of language in this context. The certainty of faith is, after all, situated in the midst of rational uncertainties and in the ambiguities of history, which are not safe from criticism. Grace, however, has a priority over existential choice; it is always prior to our act of faith. Faith can therefore persist even in a non-safe area; it can still be rationally justified and not without meaning. Reason itself operates within the mystery of the reality that is unfathomable and can never be fully rationalised.

116. In his article 'Kritisches Denken in der Theologie', F. Schupp has correctly said, in the *Zeitschrift für katholische Theologie* 92 (1970) pp 328–341, that the very fact that it is possible to study the bible using the historical critical method goes farther than a mere question of method. This comment shows that faith is situated in history.

INFORMATION ON ORIGINAL PUBLICATION

The articles collected in this volume were originally published as follows:

1 *Concilium* 5, 1 London Jan 1969, pp 22–29. Translated by Theo Westow.
2 Part of an unpublished lecture
3 *Interpretalier* 57, 1 Bussum 1969, pp. 28–56
4 *Tijdschrift voor Theologie* 9 (1969) pp 125–150
5 *ibid* 10 (1970) pp 1–22
6 *ibid* 11 (1971) pp 30–50
7 *ibid* 11 (1971) pp 113–139

INDEX